WALKING WITH
PHILIPPIANS

BECOME THE MAN GOD INTENDS YOU TO BE

Carriage
House
PUBLISHERS

A 30-DAY DEVOTIONAL
AND BIBLE STUDY

FRED J. PARRY

WALKING WITH PHILIPPIANS

Published by
Carriage House Publishers

Library of Congress Control Number: 2025901616
Paperback ISBN: 979-8-9925086-0-4
Cover Design: Debbie Lewis (Illumify Media)
Interior Design: Carolyn Preul
Copy Editor: Sandy Selby
Proofreader: Samuel P. Doherty
Printed in the United States of America

This book is dedicated to my sons, Max and Nick.

May you be blessed by the profound wisdom of the Apostle Paul,
living a life filled with purpose, love, and unwavering faith.
May you each find the strength to make your own choices and
define your lives by following the light and love that is Christ.
Let your hearts be guided by His example, and may you
inspire others as you walk in His footsteps.

With love,
Dad

CONTENTS

INTRODUCTION:
FINDING JOY AND PURPOSE

Men are struggling to find their place in the world with challenges such as identity crises, role reversals and an all-out assault on masculinity. Fortunately, the words and wisdom of the Apostle Paul from his letter to the Philippians is as timely and relevant today as it was more than 2,000 years ago. This guide to Christian living and true biblical manhood is as close as your nearest copy of the New Testament.

Many men are grappling with almost every aspect of their lives. Beyond shifts fueled by a decades-old feminist movement and an ever-changing cultural landscape, there are economic pressures and dramatic changes in personal relationships that have eroded the very definition of what it means to be a man. You can factor in the changing economic environment where men have lost motivation to complete educational pursuits, seek full-time employment and provide for their families. It's a tough time to be a man.

Studies show that men are four times more likely than women to commit suicide. For the first time in history, there are more women than men enrolled in our colleges and universities. Facing a tidal wave of discouragement, males far outpace females in the high school dropout rate. While you can make a case that the decline of men's power started as far back as the industrial revolution, it's hard to deny that the current state of manhood is in full crisis.

The good news is that the messages found in God's word can change a man's perspectives in the most positive ways. By spending a few minutes reading the Holy Bible each day, a man can gain valuable wisdom about strengthening relationships, conquering fears and setting new priorities. Once you gain a better understanding of God's true nature, you'll see how he works in people's lives for their good. You'll find that scripture can provide comfort and inspiration to steer you through life's inevitable detours.

Paul's letter to the early Christians in Philippi includes sage advice and instruction to help men reverse this decline and guide them as they strive to be more Christlike in their close relationships, work and social interactions.

Paul reminds us that adversity can strengthen our character. Philippians 4:13 tells us, "I can do all things through Christ who strengthens me." This frequently quoted verse has empowered countless men to confront their fears and difficulties. Whether you're facing challenges at work, in your relationships or in your community, you can find solace in this assurance. Embracing faith and seeking wisdom from God can provide the mental and emotional strength you need to persevere through any trial.

Another key theme in Paul's message to the Philippians is the importance of joy and purpose, regardless of circumstances. In Philippians 4:4, Paul tells us, "Rejoice in the Lord always; again, I will say, rejoice!" This instruction is profound when you consider that Paul himself was imprisoned when he wrote those words. For today's men, embracing joy can be especially challenging amid the stresses of work, finances and personal failures.

Living with purpose goes beyond simply seeking happiness; it impels us to recognize a greater calling. Men should ask themselves: What is my purpose in my job? How do I reflect my values in my family life? What legacy will I leave in my children, church and community? By cultivating a sense of purpose rooted in faith and service toward others, men can find the motivation they need to overcome any obstacle.

Another significant lesson from Paul's epistle is the emphasis on community and relationships among believers. In Philippians 1:3-5, Paul expresses gratitude for the partnership he shares with the Philippians in spreading the gospel. These words serve as an example: it's OK to accept support from other men and hold them accountable in return.

When men feel isolated or pressured to conform to societal expectations, it's beneficial to establish a brotherhood with five or six other men. These brotherly bonds foster spiritual growth and resilience. Men should aim to engage in group discussions, Bible studies or mentoring relationships to share experiences, challenges and victories. Discipleship is about guiding others and being open to learning ourselves. By actively participating in these relationships, men can inspire each other to live with integrity and purpose.

The lessons from Paul's Epistle to the Philippians offer a
compelling framework for navigating life, family and community.
By embracing joy and purpose, prioritizing family relationships,
fostering discipleship among other men and facing challenges
with faith, you will begin to build a life that honors your values
and the relationship you desire to have with God. In a world
filled with temptations, Paul's biblical principles presented in
Philippians provide a pathway to fulfillment and strength.

Fred J. Parry

MY PRAYER

Father, God, give me the discernment and clarity of mind to
receive the wisdom that Paul offers in his letter to the Philippians.
Soften my heart. Make me vulnerable so that I can make an
honest evaluation of my life today and claim the life of the man
I hope to become. Help me to find joy in my struggles, and
contentment as I build a community of believers around me.
For these things, I pray in the name of your son, Jesus Christ.
Amen.

THE MAN IN THE ARENA

"It is not the critic who counts; not the man who points out how the strong man stumbles, or where the doer of deeds could have done them better. The credit belongs to the man who is actually in the arena, whose face is marred by dust and sweat and blood; who strives valiantly; who errs, who comes short again and again, because there is no effort without error and shortcoming; but who does actually strive to do the deeds; who knows great enthusiasms, the great devotions; who spends himself in a worthy cause; who at the best knows in the end the triumph of high achievement, and who at the worst, if he fails, at least fails while daring greatly, so that his place shall never be with those cold and timid souls who neither know victory nor defeat."

— TEDDY ROOSEVELT
Excerpt from the speech "Citizenship In A Republic"
delivered at the Sorbonne, in Paris, France on April 23, 1910

HOW TO USE THIS BOOK

Walking with Philippians is designed to serve the dual purpose of being a daily devotional and a Bible study guide for Paul's Epistle to the Philippians. While the book is structured to be used over a six-week period, I would encourage you to use it at a pace that is most comfortable for you.

Each of the daily devotions is inspired by one of Paul's messages in this important letter that reminds his readers of the life and sacrifice modeled by Christ. From these messages, I have found themes that can guide us in our daily walk to become better Christians. These devotionals were written as responses from my own personal understanding of how a particular verse spoke to me. The goal of any Bible Study is to find the correct interpretation which leads to a variety of applications. That, in itself, is rightly handling the word of truth (2 Timothy 2:15).

If you're like me, you'll get a new insight or meaning each time you read one of these passages and not because the Bible's meaning has changed, but because we, as individuals, have changed since the last time we were there. We've become more aware of a different aspect of our lives, and this Scripture now speaks to us in a new way. We are more teachable than we were before. The Bible meets us where we are, and God uses His Word to lead us to greater maturity and a broader perspective. The Bible is as deep as we are and deeper still.

I would suggest approaching each devotional in prayer, asking God for clarity of mind and focus with a hope that the day's message resonates with you in some meaningful way.

Once you've read the devotional, you'll find the following tools at the end of each reading to help you get the most meaning out of the day's message:

- a reference to scripture outside Philippians that will reinforce and add context to the day's message.
- next, you'll two short questions designed to help you apply that day's lesson to your life.
- finally, you'll find a call to contemplation which is intended as a prompt for journaling. It's an excellent opportunity to explore and record your feelings as they relate to the day's message.

To gain a better understanding of the literary and cultural context of each day's passage, I would encourage you to refer to the full text each day to fully understand the contextual circumstances and events surrounding each passage.

I hope that you'll find these devotionals to be useful and relevant in your daily walk. My prayer is that the wisdom that comes from Paul's Letter to the Philippians will guide you in your journey to lead a more fulfilling and Christ-centered life.

FJP

BACKGROUND: THE APOSTLE PAUL

P aul was born in Tarsus, a major city in eastern Cilicia on the trade route between Syria and Asia Minor, in the same region as modern-day Turkey. Born the son of a Pharisee and in the ancestral lineage of the Tribe of Benjamin, Paul enjoyed the distinction of being a Jew and the privilege of being a Roman citizen. He could speak Hebrew, but his native tongue was Koine Greek. Paul studied at the prestigious rabbinical school taught by Rabbi Gamaliel, one of the most influential rabbis in the history of ancient Judaism.

Paul is among the most prominent figures in the history and growth of Christianity. He is the author of 13 of the 27 books in the New Testament. While there is scholarly debate as to the complete authenticity of some books in the New Testament, experts acknowledge that at least seven of the 13 books from Paul are undisputed as authentic works.

PAUL'S CONVERSION

Readers of the New Testament first encounter Paul as "Saul of Tarsus." Though Saul was a tentmaker by trade, he was a fervent persecutor of early Christians. In Acts 9:1-22, we read that as Saul travels from Jerusalem to Damascus during his crusade to arrest disciples, he encounters the resurrected Jesus in a brilliant light. During this experience, Jesus reveals to Saul that he is Lord and that persecuting his followers is the same as persecuting the

Lord Jesus. Saul is, in effect, fighting against God. New testament scholar N.T. Wright conjectures that during this journey, Paul was repeating a prayer used by other serious Jews in his day, requesting a visionary experience of God. An answer to that prayer was surprising enough but seeing Jesus in the place of Yahweh literally reconfigured Paul's worldview.

During this encounter, the light surrounding the vision of Jesus blinded Saul, but he traveled on to Damascus, where he remained blind for three days. Saul took no food or water for this period and stayed in a constant state of prayer until approached by a disciple named Ananias. Ananias explained that he had been sent by Jesus to restore Saul's sight and assured the blind man that the Lord would fill him with the Holy Spirit. Once Saul's sight

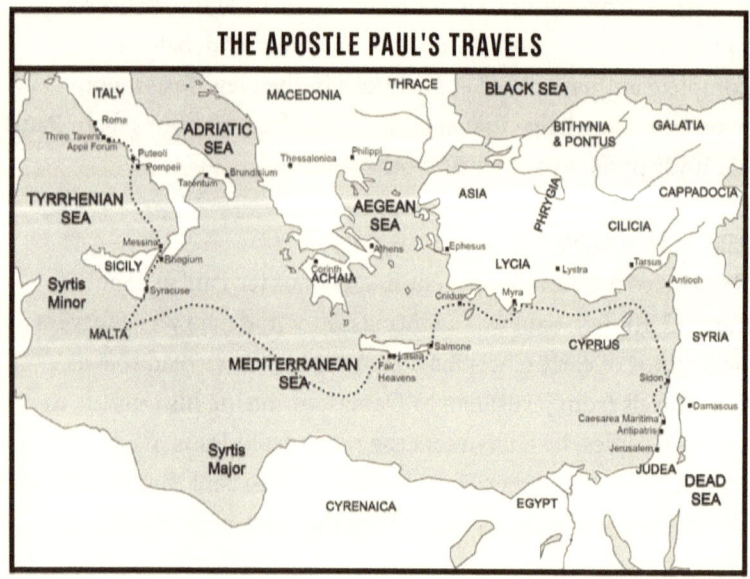

Map Copyright 2021 • Fred J. Parry

was restored, he was immediately baptized and became a fervent
believer in Jesus Christ.

PAUL'S MISSIONARY TRIPS

Following his baptism, Paul went on to Arabia and Damascus
and preached that Jesus was the Messiah. Soon thereafter, he was
persecuted for his teachings. Around A.D. 37, three years after his
conversion, Paul traveled to Jerusalem where he met for 15 days
with James, the half brother of Jesus, and the apostle Peter. Paul
used these meetings to learn more about the life of Jesus and to
report on his efforts in preaching about the Kingdom of God and
Jesus the Messiah. Over time, Paul became known as the "Apostle
to the Gentiles," while Peter would be known as the "Apostle to
the Jews."

Soon after Paul met with James and Peter, he returned to his
hometown of Tarsus to preach until Barnabas invited him to go
and teach at the rapidly growing church in Antioch. It was there
where Paul began to build a network of house churches. The
earliest Christians would gather at the homes of other followers
until the size of the group forced them to divide into smaller
groups. Antioch was also the first place where Jewish-Gentile
churches took root.

With limited resources, Paul and Barnabas often relied on the
generosity of their converts for food and housing. In A.D. 47,
Paul returned to Jerusalem with Barnabas and brought famine
relief contributed by the early churches they had started. In doing
so, Paul was, perhaps, the earliest pioneer of missionary work that
would be done by churches throughout the coming centuries.

In Acts 15, Paul and Barnabas participated in the Council of Jerusalem (circa 48-50 AD) where they met with James, Peter and John to discuss whether Gentile converts needed to be circumcised and to conform with Mosaic Law and other strict Jewish rituals. The council determined that circumcision would not be a requirement for Gentile converts to become part of God's new covenant.

Paul and Barnabas then set out from Antioch to visit Cyprus and Galatia, on the first of three mission trips. It was around this time that Saul began to be known more commonly as Paul. Historians speculate that Paul was Saul's Roman name and that the names may have been used interchangeably so that he could more easily relate to diverse audiences.

After parting ways with Barnabas in Antioch, Paul chose Silas (Silvanus) to accompany him to Syria and Cilicia to reinforce Paul's work with the churches he had previously established there. Their travels led them to Derbe and to Lystra, where they met Timothy, who was well-respected in the area. Timothy was the son of a Jewish woman and a Greek father. As the three men traveled through Phrygia and Galatia, Paul had a vision one night of a man from Macedonia pleading for them to come to that region. They departed the next morning, sailing from Troas on a course to Samothrace, Neapolis and then to Philippi.

When Paul exorcized the demons from a slave girl, he and Silas were briefly imprisoned in Philippi. Once released from captivity, they left Philippi. From there they traveled through Amphipolis and Apollonia before arriving in Thessalonica.

Thessalonica was the home of an important dockyard situated on the harbor of the Thermaic Gulf in the northwest corner of the Aegean Sea near the junction of the Egnatian Way and the road that led north to the Danube. Built by the Romans as their primary route east to Byzantium, the Egnatian Way was almost 700 miles long at the time. The roadway was nearly 20 feet wide and paved with large stone slabs topped by a hardened layer of sand. It traversed mountain passes and river gorges and provided travelers a direct connection between Rome and the Aegean Sea.

Thessalonica thrived because of its location along this major trade route to the east into Asia and west to Rome. It became a city known for its prosperity and cultural activity. Located 100 miles southwest of Philippi, Thessalonica eventually became the capital of the Roman province of Macedon. Thessalonica was a thriving city of nearly 200,000 citizens in Macedonia in Northern Greece. The city still exists but is now known as Thessaloniki.

Paul's trip to Thessalonica was significant because it marked the beginning of the gospel's spread from Asia to Europe. Tragically, Paul's time in Thessalonica was cut short by mob-led persecution. He fled the region and traveled on to Berea, but angry mobs there forced him to move on to Athens for a brief time. Paul eventually settled in Corinth.

In 1 Corinthians 2:3, we learn that Paul had become fearful and discouraged with the fruits of his missionary work. He deeply regretted leaving his new believers before they were established in their faith. The imprisonment, persecution, and treatment by angry mobs had taken a toll on Paul. He was concerned about the churches he had planted and worried about their viability. While in Berea, Paul sent Silas and Timothy back to Thessalonica to check on that new church.

THE CAPTIVITY EPISTLES

Throughout his ministry life, Paul was jailed on numerous occasions and placed under house arrest for extended periods. It was during these periods that Paul crafted several letters to churches he had planted. Because Paul wrote these letters while imprisoned, they are often referred to as the "Captivity Epistles."

In Acts 16:16-34, while Paul and Silas were imprisoned in Philippi, an earthquake brought down the walls of the jail. Paul and Silas made the conscious decision not to escape, and this led to a trusting relationship with their jailer, who became a follower of Christ. In A.D. 57, Paul returned to Jerusalem and was soon arrested and jailed for taking a Gentile too far into the precincts of the temple. These were false accusations based on faulty assumptions, but they caused enough upheaval to gain the attention of Roman authorities (Acts 22:29).

During his captivity in Jerusalem, Paul defended his actions before the Sanhedrin. His testimony divided the Sadducees and Pharisees who had strong disagreements over whether Paul had broken any laws. Roman authorities then took Paul, with an armed escort, to Caesarea for higher officials to hear the case. Paul remained there for several years and despite his innocence, he was not released. Biblical tradition reports that a Roman official was trying to extort a bribe from him in exchange for his release, but Paul refused (Acts 24:26). Finally, exasperated, Paul asked to make an appeal to Caesar himself. After his request was reluctantly granted, Paul was placed on a ship as a prisoner to sail to Rome. On that voyage, he was shipwrecked on the island of Malta for three months where he performed miracles and continued to preach the word of God.

When Paul finally arrived in Rome, he was placed under house arrest but allowed to continue preaching without interruption from authorities. During this time, Paul wrote his letters to the Philippians, Ephesians, Colossians, and Philemon. After his release, it is believed Paul traveled to Spain, where he wrote his letters to Timothy and Titus.

PAUL'S DEATH SENTENCE

In A.D. 64, Paul returned to Rome where he was martyred. While little has been written regarding the details surrounding Paul's death, tradition has it that Roman Emperor Nero sentenced him to death. Paul's death sentence came shortly after a large portion of Rome, filled mostly with tenements for the poor, burned. Nero blamed the fire on Christians, although Roman documents suggest that Nero started the fire himself to clear the area for a building project.

Because Paul was a Roman citizen, he was exempt from death by crucifixion. Instead, he was decapitated by a sword. In the end, Paul died because of his faith. In his final writings, it was clear that he was ready and willing to die for Christ. Paul gave his last breath for the cause of helping the first generation of Christians understand that sacrifice was an integral part of following Christ.

FJP

BACKGROUND: PAUL'S LETTER TO PHILIPPIANS

The Epistle to the Philippians is one of the most personal and affectionate letters penned by the Apostle Paul. It reflects his deep bond with the Christian community in Philippi. Most scholars date this letter to around AD 60-62, while Paul was in prison, likely in Rome. This letter reveals valuable insights about Paul's visits to Philippi, his relationship with its people, and the challenges he faced there. The themes presented in this letter are similar to those found in Paul's other messages in the broader context of the New Testament.

PAUL'S VISITS TO PHILIPPI

Paul first visited Philippi during his second missionary journey, which is detailed in Acts 16:11-40. This visit occurred around AD 49-50. Upon arriving, Paul and his companions, including Silas and Timothy, sought out a gathering of Jews who were in prayer at the river. There they encountered Lydia, a wealthy seller of purple cloth and one of their first converts.

Paul and his companions experienced notable success in establishing the church in Philippi. Their ministry also sparked conflict. After Paul cast evil spirits out of a slave girl, her owners had Paul and Silas arrested and imprisoned. While in jail, an earthquake caused the jail walls to collapse. Paul and Silas did not flee and turned themselves in to the jailer. The event led to the jailer's conversion and brought them one step closer to solidifying the church's foundation in Philippi.

ABOUT PHILIPPI

Philippi, a prominent city located in Macedonia, was known for its Roman heritage and for being a military colony. At the time of Paul's writings, it was the leading center of culture and commerce in the region. Located approximately 10 miles north of Annapolis harbor on the Aegean Sea along the Egnatian Way, it was originally settled by Philip II of Macedon, the father of Alexander the Great, after he conquered the village of Thrace and named the area for himself. The area featured fertile agriculture land and was largely populated by farmers and peasants of Greek and Roman descent.

In many respects, Philippi was a miniature version of a Roman City. With a population of 10,000, it was under the governance of the Roman Empire, unlike surrounding cities. Citizens of Philippi were not required to pay taxes, and they were allowed to own land, which was an unusual privilege. Philippi was later the site of a significant battle during the Roman Civil War and was eventually resettled by the assassins of Julius Caesar, Mark Anthony and Octavian.

RELATIONSHIP WITH THE PEOPLE OF PHILIPPI

Paul's relationship with the Philippians was characterized by warmth, gratitude, and mutual support. The Philippian church became known for its generosity and support for Paul's ministry, even while he was imprisoned. In Philippians 4:15-16, Paul expresses his gratitude and acknowledges their financial contributions. Their support not only bolstered Paul's work but also demonstrated the Philippians' commitment to the Gospel.

The bond between Paul and the Philippians was deeply personal. He expresses joy and affection for them throughout the letter, using terms of endearment such as "my beloved" (Philippians 4:1). This emotional connection is indicative of the significant role the Philippians played in Paul's life and ministry, serving as a source of encouragement and strength amid his trials.

FALSE TEACHERS AND JUDAIZERS

Despite the initial success of the mission in Philippi, Paul encountered considerable opposition. The social dynamics in Philippi were complex. Although Paul had both strong ties to Roman citizenship and a Jewish heritage, he still came up against a reluctance to embrace the new sect of Judaism and Christianity that he represented.

After Paul's departure, reports indicated that the Philippian church faced difficulties, including internal strife and external persecution (Philippians 1:27-30). There were many false teachers who worked diligently to discredit Paul and misinform these new Christians on the necessity of staying true to Mosaic Law. To complicate matters, Paul faced potential divisions within the church, prompting him to teach about unity and humility in the face of adversity (Philippians 2:1-4).

SIGNIFICANCE OF THE LETTER

Paul's letter to the Philippians includes themes of joy, unity, humility and perseverance that resonate throughout the text.

This letter serves as a guide to living as a mature Christian. Among the salient features of this letter is the prominent Christological hymn (also known as the Christ Poem) found in Philippians 2:5-11, which highlights the humility and exaltation of Jesus and serves as a model for Christian conduct. Here is that hymn:

In your relationships with one another, have the same mindset as Christ Jesus:
> Who, being in very nature God,
>   did not consider equality with God
> something to be used to his own advantage;
> rather, he made himself nothing
>   by taking the very nature of a servant,
>   being made in human likeness.
> And being found in appearance as a man,
>   he humbled himself
>   by becoming obedient to death—
>   even death on a cross!
> Therefore God exalted him to the highest place
>   and gave him the name that is above every name,
> that at the name of Jesus every knee should bow,
>   in heaven and on earth and under the earth,
> and every tongue acknowledge that Jesus Christ is Lord,
>   to the glory of God the Father.

Paul's letter to the Philippians serves important purposes including a theological reflection into the Pauline theology views on salvation, faith and the transformative power of Christ in a believer's life. Paul gives encouragement and reassurance to his readers who have suffered through persecution and hardship. Paul stresses the need to rejoice always, regardless of the circumstances, and he instructs his readers to focus on building community through activities that support and engage the entire community.

PAUL'S EPISTLE TO THE PHILIPPIANS

PHILIPPIANS 1

Paul and Timothy, servants of Christ Jesus,
To all God's holy people in Christ Jesus at Philippi, together with the overseers and deacons:
² Grace and peace to you from God our Father and the Lord Jesus Christ.

THANKSGIVING AND PRAYER

³ I thank my God every time I remember you. ⁴ In all my prayers for all of you, I always pray with joy ⁵ because of your partnership in the gospel from the first day until now, ⁶ being confident of this, that he who began a good work in you will carry it on to completion until the day of Christ Jesus.

⁷ It is right for me to feel this way about all of you, since I have you in my heart and, whether I am in chains or defending and confirming the gospel, all of you share in God's grace with me. ⁸ God can testify how I long for all of you with the affection of Christ Jesus.

⁹ And this is my prayer: that your love may abound more and more in knowledge and depth of insight, ¹⁰ so that you may be able to discern what is best and may be pure and blameless for the day of Christ, ¹¹ filled with the fruit of righteousness that comes through Jesus Christ—to the glory and praise of God.

PAUL'S CHAINS ADVANCE THE GOSPEL

[12] Now I want you to know, brothers and sisters, that what has happened to me has actually served to advance the gospel. [13] As a result, it has become clear throughout the whole palace guard and to everyone else that I am in chains for Christ. [14] And because of my chains, most of the brothers and sisters have become confident in the Lord and dare all the more to proclaim the gospel without fear.

[15] It is true that some preach Christ out of envy and rivalry, but others out of goodwill. [16] The latter do so out of love, knowing that I am put here for the defense of the gospel. [17] The former preach Christ out of selfish ambition, not sincerely, supposing that they can stir up trouble for me while I am in chains. [18] But what does it matter? The important thing is that in every way, whether from false motives or true, Christ is preached. And because of this I rejoice.

Yes, and I will continue to rejoice, [19] for I know that through your prayers and God's provision of the Spirit of Jesus Christ what has happened to me will turn out for my deliverance. [20] I eagerly expect and hope that I will in no way be ashamed, but will have sufficient courage so that now as always Christ will be exalted in my body, whether by life or by death. [21] For to me, to live is Christ and to die is gain. [22] If I am to go on living in the body, this will mean fruitful labor for me. Yet what shall I choose? I do not know! [23] I am torn between the two: I desire to depart and be with Christ, which is better by far; [24] but it is more necessary for you that I remain in the body. [25] Convinced of this, I know that I will remain, and I will continue with all of you for your progress and joy in the faith, [26] so that through my being with you again your boasting in Christ Jesus will abound on account of me.

LIFE WORTHY OF THE GOSPEL

[27] Whatever happens, conduct yourselves in a manner worthy of the gospel of Christ. Then, whether I come and see you or only hear about you in my absence, I will know that you stand firm in the one Spirit, striving together as one for the faith of the gospel [28] without being frightened in any way by those who oppose you. This is a sign to them that they will be destroyed, but that you will be saved—and that by God. [29] For it has been granted to you on behalf of Christ not only to believe in him, but also to suffer for him, [30] since you are going through the same struggle you saw I had, and now hear that I still have.

PHILIPPIANS 2

IMITATING CHRIST'S HUMILITY

Therefore if you have any encouragement from being united with Christ, if any comfort from his love, if any common sharing in the Spirit, if any tenderness and compassion, [2] then make my joy complete by being like-minded, having the same love, being one in spirit and of one mind. [3] Do nothing out of selfish ambition or vain conceit. Rather, in humility value others above yourselves, [4] not looking to your own interests but each of you to the interests of the others.

[5] In your relationships with one another, have the same mindset as Christ Jesus:

[6] Who, being in very nature God,
   did not consider equality with God something to be used to
   his own advantage;
[7] rather, he made himself nothing
      by taking the very nature of a servant,
      being made in human likeness.
[8] And being found in appearance as a man,
   he humbled himself
   by becoming obedient to death—
      even death on a cross!
[9] Therefore God exalted him to the highest place
   and gave him the name that is above every name,
[10] that at the name of Jesus every knee should bow,
   in heaven and on earth and under the earth,
[11] and every tongue acknowledge that Jesus Christ is Lord,
   to the glory of God the Father.

DO EVERYTHING WITHOUT GRUMBLING

[12] Therefore, my dear friends, as you have always obeyed—not
only in my presence, but now much more in my absence—
continue to work out your salvation with fear and trembling, [13] for
it is God who works in you to will and to act in order to fulfill his
good purpose.

[14] Do everything without grumbling or arguing, [15] so that you may
become blameless and pure, "children of God without fault in
a warped and crooked generation." Then you will shine among
them like stars in the sky [16] as you hold firmly to the word of life.
And then I will be able to boast on the day of Christ that I did
not run or labor in vain. [17] But even if I am being poured out like

a drink offering on the sacrifice and service coming from your faith, I am glad and rejoice with all of you. [18] So you too should be glad and rejoice with me.

TIMOTHY AND EPAPHRODITUS

[19] I hope in the Lord Jesus to send Timothy to you soon, that I also may be cheered when I receive news about you. [20] I have no one else like him, who will show genuine concern for your welfare. [21] For everyone looks out for their own interests, not those of Jesus Christ. [22] But you know that Timothy has proved himself, because as a son with his father he has served with me in the work of the gospel. [23] I hope, therefore, to send him as soon as I see how things go with me. [24] And I am confident in the Lord that I myself will come soon.

[25] But I think it is necessary to send back to you Epaphroditus, my brother, co-worker and fellow soldier, who is also your messenger, whom you sent to take care of my needs. [26] For he longs for all of you and is distressed because you heard he was ill. [27] Indeed he was ill, and almost died. But God had mercy on him, and not on him only but also on me, to spare me sorrow upon sorrow. [28] Therefore I am all the more eager to send him, so that when you see him again you may be glad and I may have less anxiety. [29] So then, welcome him in the Lord with great joy, and honor people like him, [30] because he almost died for the work of Christ. He risked his life to make up for the help you yourselves could not give me.

PHILIPPIANS 3

NO CONFIDENCE IN THE FLESH

Further, my brothers and sisters, rejoice in the Lord! It is no trouble for me to write the same things to you again, and it is a safeguard for you. [2] Watch out for those dogs, those evildoers, those mutilators of the flesh. [3] For it is we who are the circumcision, we who serve God by his Spirit, who boast in Christ Jesus, and who put no confidence in the flesh— 4 though I myself have reasons for such confidence.

If someone else thinks they have reasons to put confidence in the flesh, I have more: [5] circumcised on the eighth day, of the people of Israel, of the tribe of Benjamin, a Hebrew of Hebrews; in regard to the law, a Pharisee; [6] as for zeal, persecuting the church; as for righteousness based on the law, faultless.

[7] But whatever were gains to me I now consider loss for the sake of Christ. [8] What is more, I consider everything a loss because of the surpassing worth of knowing Christ Jesus my Lord, for whose sake I have lost all things. I consider them garbage, that I may gain Christ [9] and be found in him, not having a righteousness of my own that comes from the law, but that which is through faith in Christ—the righteousness that comes from God on the basis of faith. [10] I want to know Christ—yes, to know the power of his resurrection and participation in his sufferings, becoming like him in his death, [11] and so, somehow, attaining to the resurrection from the dead.

[12] Not that I have already obtained all this, or have already arrived at my goal, but I press on to take hold of that for which Christ Jesus took hold of me. [13] Brothers and sisters, I do not consider

myself yet to have taken hold of it. But one thing I do: Forgetting what is behind and straining toward what is ahead, ¹⁴ I press on toward the goal to win the prize for which God has called me heavenward in Christ Jesus.

FOLLOWING PAUL'S EXAMPLE

¹⁵ All of us, then, who are mature should take such a view of things. And if on some point you think differently, that too God will make clear to you. ¹⁶ Only let us live up to what we have already attained.

¹⁷ Join together in following my example, brothers and sisters, and just as you have us as a model, keep your eyes on those who live as we do. ¹⁸ For, as I have often told you before and now tell you again even with tears, many live as enemies of the cross of Christ. ¹⁹ Their destiny is destruction, their god is their stomach, and their glory is in their shame. Their mind is set on earthly things. ²⁰ But our citizenship is in heaven. And we eagerly await a Savior from there, the Lord Jesus Christ, ²¹ who, by the power that enables him to bring everything under his control, will transform our lowly bodies so that they will be like his glorious body.

PHILIPPIANS 4

CLOSING APPEAL FOR STEADFASTNESS AND UNITY

Therefore, my brothers and sisters, you whom I love and long for, my joy and crown, stand firm in the Lord in this way, dear friends!

² I plead with Euodia and I plead with Syntyche to be of the same mind in the Lord. ³ Yes, and I ask you, my true companion, help

these women since they have contended at my side in the cause of the gospel, along with Clement and the rest of my co-workers, whose names are in the book of life.

FINAL EXHORTATIONS

[4] Rejoice in the Lord always. I will say it again: Rejoice! [5] Let your gentleness be evident to all. The Lord is near. [6] Do not be anxious about anything, but in every situation, by prayer and petition, with thanksgiving, present your requests to God. [7] And the peace of God, which transcends all understanding, will guard your hearts and your minds in Christ Jesus.

[8] Finally, brothers and sisters, whatever is true, whatever is noble, whatever is right, whatever is pure, whatever is lovely, whatever is admirable—if anything is excellent or praiseworthy—think about such things. [9] Whatever you have learned or received or heard from me, or seen in me—put it into practice. And the God of peace will be with you.

THANKS FOR THEIR GIFTS

[10] I rejoiced greatly in the Lord that at last you renewed your concern for me. Indeed, you were concerned, but you had no opportunity to show it. [11] I am not saying this because I am in need, for I have learned to be content whatever the circumstances. [12] I know what it is to be in need, and I know what it is to have plenty. I have learned the secret of being content in any and every situation, whether well fed or hungry, whether living in plenty or in want. [13] I can do all this through him who gives me strength.

[14] Yet it was good of you to share in my troubles. [15] Moreover, as you Philippians know, in the early days of your acquaintance with the gospel, when I set out from Macedonia, not one church shared with me in the matter of giving and receiving, except you only; [16] for even when I was in Thessalonica, you sent me aid more than once when I was in need. [17] Not that I desire your gifts; what I desire is that more be credited to your account. [18] I have received full payment and have more than enough. I am amply supplied, now that I have received from Epaphroditus the gifts you sent. They are a fragrant offering, an acceptable sacrifice, pleasing to God. [19] And my God will meet all your needs according to the riches of his glory in Christ Jesus.

[20] To our God and Father be glory for ever and ever. Amen.

FINAL GREETINGS

[21] Greet all God's people in Christ Jesus. The brothers and sisters who are with me send greetings. [22] All God's people here send you greetings, especially those who belong to Caesar's household. [23] The grace of the Lord Jesus Christ be with your spirit. Amen.

And because of my chains, most of the brothers
and sisters have become confident in the Lord and dare
all the more to proclaim the gospel without fear."

Philippians 1:14 NIV

WEEK 1

THE GOOD WORK

"In all my prayers for all of you, I always pray with joy because of your partnership in the gospel from the first day until now." Philippians 1:4-5 NIV

I remember my early attempts to learn the craft of fly fishing. Despite my best efforts, I could not pick up the subtleties of the sport on my own. I hired a guide to take me to a spot where I could practice casting and mending without the judgment of other anglers. My guide earned his keep that first day, spending hours trying to remove my tangled flies from the thickets along the riverbank. Though my skills gradually improved throughout the day, I still ended up with a bird's nest of knots in my line as I tried to set my fly gently on the current. I would require several more seasons of practice before I got the hang of fly fishing. I was making progress, but it was slow.

In Paul's letter to Philippi, he shares his elation over the progress these new Christians are making in their spiritual journeys, but he points out that God's work in their lives was just beginning. While God had begun the good work with their salvation, their continued spiritual development would require a considerable effort. Their Christian walks would bring the satisfaction of growing closer to God, but they had to continue investing in their efforts to become more Christlike. Paul assured these Christians that they would have the benefit of the Holy Spirit to guide them on their journey.

Like with fly fishing, becoming a mature Christian takes a lot of work to sustain your momentum. What does spiritual development look like in your life? Perhaps it's being intentional about spending time in God's word every single day. Maybe it will involve surrounding yourself with a small group of like-minded believers who will join you in studying God's word and encouraging you in your walk. Perhaps your spiritual growth will come from serving in your church or community. Whatever path you choose, your journey will include forward motions and disappointing setbacks. One thing is certain—your work will bring you closer to God and the gift of eternal life he has promised to you.

MY PRAYER

God, give me the encouragement I need to be steadfast in my journey toward you. Help me be intentional in pursuing you through your word and in my service to others. May I always keep my eyes focused on the reward of an eternal life with you. I pray for these things in the name of your son, Jesus Christ. Amen.

READ: 2 CORINTHIANS 5:17

QUESTION 1: What steps can you take daily to grow spiritually in Christ?

QUESTION 2: Who are the people in your life you could ask to walk alongside you in this journey?

CONTEMPLATE

Write a prayer asking God to guide you in your spiritual walk. Where do you need the most help? How can you lean into the Holy Spirit to ensure your success?

SANCTIFICATION

"Being confident of this, that he who began a good work in you will carry it on to completion until the day of Christ Jesus." Philippians 1:6 NIV

When you decide to follow Jesus, a process of transformation begins that will slowly change your life. You may not notice the gradual changes, but you are still changing. Know that God has begun a good work in you, and he won't quit until the job is finished. I had hoped that on the day of my baptism at age 45, I was going to come out of that pool of water as a new man. I desperately wanted to be changed, free from the sinful temptations of lust, greed and gluttony. As I look back on the stages of my spiritual journey, I can see now how God was changing me. It was a slow and steady process. Over the course of many years, God put new people in my life, created new opportunities for me to pursue, and challenged me in ways I could have never imagined.

Sanctification is best described as an ongoing process where your life becomes more aligned with the words, thoughts and actions of Jesus. The Holy Spirit works within you to transform the way you think, speak and treat others. Your character evolves to make you more holy, compassionate and selfless. You can't control the process. You can only participate in the sense that you are eagerly receiving the transformational work God is doing in your life by following his teachings and abiding by his will. Like a rough stone that has been placed into a rock tumbler, your life is gradually becoming more precious and valuable. You are the diamond still in the rough.

While the salvation of the early Christians in Philippi is secure, Paul encourages them to let the process of sanctification run its course as they share the gospel, promote justice and reflect God's love while serving others. As humans, we desperately want to be in control of the things that affect and shape our lives. Only God can do the transformative work being done. Let God use you in this process. Be ready to surrender your selfish desires and be prepared to say "YES" to what God has planned. Our outward obedience will begin with an inward love for Jesus.

MY PRAYER

Heavenly Father, give me the wisdom to accept the things you have planned for my life. Help me to be obedient and supple as you transform me into something that only you could have created. Give me the patience I need so that I may see what your masterpiece will eventually become. For these things, I pray in the name of your son, Jesus Christ. Amen.

READ: 2 TIMOTHY 2:21

QUESTION #1: In what ways have you seen the process of sanctification work its way through your life?

QUESTION #2: How has God changed you as a result of this process?

CONTEMPLATE

Write a letter to your future self that expresses your hopes for what your transformed life will look like. Write about the ways in which you hope your heart will be changed. Write about the parts of your life you hope will not change.

A PURE LIFE

"...so that you may be able to discern what is best and may be pure and blameless for the day of Christ," Philippians 1:10 NIV

One of my favorite places in the world to visit is Costa Rica. No matter where you go in the Central American country, you'll hear a common greeting: pura vida. Pura vida translates into English as "pure life" or "simple life," but it is more than simple words. This phrase encourages recipients to appreciate life, slow down, and embrace gratitude for all they have. They are valuable words that can shape your perspective. In our culture, we often think the words "pure life" are a reference to sexual purity. Though a great number of men struggle with purity, Paul is referring to being pure in the way you live your life as a follower of Christ.

What does living a pure life as a godly man look like these days? Paul encourages us to pursue the level of quality in our daily lives that honors God in all we do. Initially, the idea of such purity may seem unattainable, but the goal is to conduct ourselves in a way where every breath we take and thought we make is focused on serving our loving God. Living a pure life means resisting every form of temptation and source of evil that lurks in hidden corners. Paul reminds us that as we grow in our love for God and others, our goal is to become morally pure and blameless. Our pursuit of a pure life is a journey and, like so many other journeys, is filled with pitfalls, setbacks and unexpected detours. The key is to keep moving forward.

Living a pure life may require you to hit a reset button in your life. The first step may require assuming a posture of gentleness, which may not be one of your strongest characteristics. Being gentle means allowing the peace of Christ to rule in your heart and letting his word seep into your innermost being. With a spirit of humility, take a moment to think before you speak and to pause before you react to the actions of others. Consider whether your actions and words reflect the face of God. Lastly, be intentional in your good works without the expectation of anything in return or anyone noticing your efforts. God will bless you with his favor when you pursue a pure life.

MY PRAYER

God, grant me the discipline and obedience to pursue a pure life that honors you. Let me be mindful and intentional in my words and actions, weighing them by the value they offer those around me. Help me make choices that are aligned with a pure heart. I pray for these things in the name of your son, Jesus Christ. Amen.

READ: PSALMS 101:2-5

QUESTION #1: In what areas of your life do you need to pursue a purer life?

QUESTION #2: What steps can you take to live more gently?

CONTEMPLATE

Make a list of the things in your life that do not demonstrate a pure life. Which of these things are a priority for you to change? What specific steps will you take immediately to pursue a purer life?

CAPTIVE AUDIENCE

"Now I want you to know, brothers and sisters, that what has happened to me has actually served to advance the gospel. As a result, it has become clear throughout the whole palace guard and to everyone else that I am in chains for Christ. And because of my chains, most of the brothers and sisters have become confident in the Lord and dare all the more to proclaim the gospel without fear." Philippians 1:12-14 NIV

You've heard the saying, "When the world gives you lemons, make lemonade." In other words, transform what normally would be a disadvantage into a positive outcome. Some of us have plenty of experience dealing with lemons. The Apostle Paul was masterful at turning something negative into something positive. When he wrote his letter to the Philippians, he was under house arrest in Rome. He literally was chained to one of the emperor's personal bodyguards. The fact that Paul was held captive by members of the Praetorian Guard was a sign of his status as a prisoner and the threat his message represented to the government.

Because Paul was under constant watch while awaiting trial, he had an opportunity to influence the guards by sharing the gospel with them. The guards could hear him pray, worship and speak with gentleness to others. They were undoubtedly impressed by his loyalty to Christ and with the deep conviction of his beliefs. Paul reported that one by one, the guards began to accept Christ and become believers. Because Paul was so bold in his faith, he seized every opportunity to advance the gospel and use his hardship to further God's work. The influential Praetorian Guard would, in turn, further spread the word of God. Ironically, this is the exact crime for which Paul was being held. Paul had a captive audience and made the most of his difficult circumstances.

What if you could imitate Paul's actions in your daily life? What captive audiences are you exposed to on a regular basis? We spend time every day with our family members and co-workers. Don't we have the same opportunity to spread the gospel to these audiences?

By deepening our relationships with others, we can discover their genuine needs, then demonstrate our Christian values and show them how our relationship with God fulfills our needs. It starts with being a good listener and then integrating faith into our conversations with them. When we show our compassion, kindness and forgiveness in our interactions with others, we inadvertently teach others about Christ. These relationships take time to build and are only solidified when we have earned trust. Be patient but confident, knowing that in all things God works for the good of those who love and believe in him.

MY PRAYER

God, help me to recognize the captive audiences in my life and then give me the courage to spread the gospel. Give me the confidence to be bold in my faith. For these things, I pray in the name of your son, Jesus Christ. Amen.

READ: MATTHEW 28:19

QUESTION 1: In what part of your life do you have captive audiences in which to spread the gospel?

QUESTION 2: How confident are you in your ability to tell another person about the reasons to follow Christ? What can you do to strengthen your discipleship skills?

CONTEMPLATE

Write out the words you would use to tell a co-worker or family member about Christ. What parts of your faith journey would you incorporate into the story? How would you tell them about the ways God has changed your life?

CHECKING YOUR MOTIVATION

"It is true that some preach Christ out of envy and rivalry, but others out of goodwill." Philippians 1:15 NIV

Have you ever had a boss say, "I don't care how you get the job done as long as you get it done"? By almost any interpretation, those instructions indicate little concern for the method or process in which the work is done. The most important concern is that the job is finished. If you've been on this planet long enough, you know that there are two types of workers in the workplace. One group will perform a task to the highest quality standards possible while others just check the boxes and punch the time clock with little pride in workmanship. Sometimes the motivation behind the way we work doesn't matter. Paul was quick to make this distinction when considering the motivation behind false teachers.

In Philippi, there were those teaching God's word for the sole purpose of gaining status and influence in the Christian community. Some were motivated by the opportunity to discredit Paul and his previous teachings. Paul made it clear that he was happy that God's word was being taught, regardless of the teachers' motivations. As long as the truth was preached, Paul didn't care that some teachers were mocking him out of jealousy or to get under his skin while he was imprisoned in Rome. In our spiritual walks, it's always a good idea to consider the motivations behind the relationship we desire with Christ.

Are you someone who is seeking God's favor, or are you instead seeking the approval of other men? Pursuing God requires a selfless mindset and posture. Seeking the favor of man may mean saying and doing whatever it takes to advance your stature. As a result, so many of the human relationships we have forged over the years are purely transactional. That's not the case with God because you have nothing to offer God. Everything you have already belongs to him. God knows your darkest secrets and he still loves you. God also knows the motives behind the things you say and do. Now is the time to get your motivations in check. You can begin by living a life that honors God by serving and loving those around you. Do it for the right reasons. Do it for God.

MY PRAYER

Father, God, give me the discernment needed to check my motivations. Let me be driven by the need to live my life in a way that brings you honor. Help me recognize the sin of doing things for the wrong reasons. Let me be earnest in my desire to be transparent and unashamedly bold in my allegiance to you. For these things, I pray in the name of your son, Jesus Christ. Amen.

READ: LUKE 18:10-14

QUESTION 1: In what aspects of your life do you need to reevaluate your motivations?

QUESTION 2: How would you best describe your motivations for following Christ?

CONTEMPLATE

Write a prayer that outlines your motivations and reasons for following Christ. Acknowledge your past transgressions where your motives may not have been pure. What steps will you take to correct your path?

"For to me, to live is Christ and to die is gain."

Philippians 1:21 NIV

WEEK 2

NO REGRETS

"I eagerly expect and hope that I will in no way be ashamed, but will have sufficient courage so that now as always Christ will be exalted in my body, whether by life or by death." Philippians 1:20 NIV

Have you ever done something so well that you have zero regrets about the experience? Perhaps you trained for a marathon and surprised yourself with the results on race day. Maybe you completed a DIY construction project that far exceeded your expectations. You might be one of those guys who invested 110% effort in doing his job and retired with confidence that you gave the job your best. There aren't a lot of situations in our lives where we have no regrets about the way things came together. Humility aside, we don't always give things our best effort. We know we could have done something a bit better or worked a little harder. The Apostle Paul didn't share the same concern. He knew that he had done his best and had no shame in saying so.

As Paul's trial before Caesar grew near, he knew that the end of his life could be at hand. Without fear or hesitation, Paul was confident that his work for God's kingdom had been done to the best of his ability. If death was to be the outcome, Paul knew that it was simply a transition. He had honored God with his life and ministry, and the manner in which he died would also honor Christ. Either way, Paul would be united with Christ because he had honored him in all circumstances.

I think most of us would love the opportunity to reach the end of our lives and look back with no regrets. To accomplish this, we would be wise to model our lives after Paul. Living like Paul begins with demonstrating an unshakable love and compassion for everyone we meet. Without judgment or hesitation, we would humble ourselves and find ways to serve all those we encounter, regardless of their societal status, heritage or previous sins. We would show an unwavering commitment to God's word, pursuing him without abandon. We would embrace our hardships and recognize the opportunities for growth they bring.

Paul lived a sacrificial life, but he knew the final reward was great. In the end, he died as a martyr without regret for his commitment to Christ. He died confident that he had an eternal home because of a life well-lived.

MY PRAYER

God, show me how to surrender in obedience to living a life that mirrors the life of the Apostle Paul. Give me his steadfast nature, his unyielding principle and his focus on the ultimate prize. I pray for these things in the name of your son, Jesus Christ. Amen.

READ: ACTS 18:1-17

QUESTION 1: What are the characteristics of the Apostle Paul that you would like to imitate?

QUESTION 2: What is a characteristic of Paul that you believe would be the hardest to emulate?

CONTEMPLATE

Write a journal entry that describes what it might feel like to have no regrets at the end of your life on this earth. What things will you re-prioritize in your life? How will this affect existing relationships?

TO DIE IS GAIN

"For to me, to live is Christ and to die is gain. If I am to go on living in the body, this will mean fruitful labor for me. Yet what shall I choose? I do not know! I am torn between the two: I desire to depart and be with Christ, which is better by far." Philippians 1:21-23 NIV

To die is gain. That's not a phrase you hear often these days. For most of us, death seems like the worst possible outcome in almost any scenario. When we first learn of the passing of a friend, acquaintance or loved one, we feel a sense of loss. Grief settles over us. When my wife became gravely ill a couple of years ago, I was overwhelmed by the fear that she might die of her illness. When she did pass away a few weeks later, I hated death. I felt cheated and robbed of the decades we were supposed to have together. As I have traveled my circuitous journey through grief, I now see her death as something different. Despite my personal loss, I have found peace knowing that my wife is experiencing the joy of being in the constant presence of Jesus. She has received her eternal reward and, while I miss her terribly, I know that she is in a much better place.

To live or die was a complicated juxtaposition for Paul. His life on this earth was one of great sacrifice. He had suffered. It was unlikely that his persecution at the hands of his enemies was going to subside, yet he knew that it all had a divine purpose. Paul's trials brought him a degree of joy because he knew something positive was coming from his hardships. Paul also knew that should his imprisonment ultimately end with his death, he would be in the presence of Jesus. Paul was just as enthused about continuing his work on this earth as he was in earning his final reward at the feet of Jesus.

Our culture has an unhealthy perspective about death. Like suffering, it's just part of life. No matter how hard we try, we can't escape it, so why not embrace it? If you've accepted Jesus, sought the forgiveness of your sins and made him the leader of your life, you'll discover one day that death ain't so bad. We should strive to live our lives in a manner consistent with the Apostle Paul. To compare the joy of serving others against living in the paradise with God says something powerful and poignant about his perspective. We can't escape death, so why not spend the rest of our living days building up our treasures in heaven?

MY PRAYER

Father, God, I pray that I can find the joy that Paul found in serving others and growing your kingdom. Let me live my life in such a way that I can eagerly await the eternal reward you have promised. Help me remember that my home is not on this earth but in heaven with you. I pray for these things in the name of your son, Jesus Christ. Amen.

READ: JAMES 1:12

QUESTION #1: What do you dread the most about your own death?

QUESTION #2: Are you confident you will receive the eternal reward God has offered you through salvation?

CONTEMPLATE

Write a letter to yourself from someone close to you who has died. In this letter, have them describe the wonders of heaven as you might imagine. Have them describe how heaven compares to our life on this earth.

LIVING CONSISTENTLY

"Whatever happens, conduct yourselves in a manner worthy of the gospel of Christ. Then, whether I come and see you or only hear about you in my absence, I will know that you stand firm in the one Spirit, striving together as one for the faith of the gospel." Philippians 1:27 NIV

Are you the same person on Sunday morning that you are on Friday night? Most of us aren't. It's common to have one foot planted in your old life while the other foot dips its toes into the life you wish you were living. You can't have it both ways. The people with whom you surround yourself can make all the difference. I'm not saying you have to get rid of all your friends from back when you were "fun," but you may need to set new boundaries for yourself and for those with whom you spend time.

In Romans 12:2, the Apostle Paul tells us, "Do not conform to the pattern of this world, but be transformed by the renewing of your mind." Ponder these words. God is creating an opening for us. Instead of being trapped in the isolation and sin that was your old life, God is inviting you to discover something truly transformative. He wants you to be happy and filled with joy. He wants you to live in communion with him and enjoy a fulfilling life until you can join him in eternity.

Paul calls on us to live in a way that reflects the messages of Christ. By aligning ourselves with the teachings of the gospel, we will live with love, humility and integrity. To be successful, we need to surround ourselves with people who live the same way. We need friends who will hold us accountable, ask us tough questions, support us when we're vulnerable, and encourage us when we think we're going to fail.

Pursuing a spiritually rewarding life won't be easy, but it will be worth any struggle.

MY PRAYER

Father, God, help me to be mindful of your call to live with love, integrity and compassion. Give me the discipline to live consistently in a manner that reflects the teachings of the Gospel. Let me become more and more like Christ with each passing day. For these things I pray in the name of Jesus. Amen.

READ: ROMANS 12:2

QUESTION #1: When is your behavior more likely to be inconsistent with how you act on Sunday mornings at church?

QUESTION #2: What is one aspect of your behavior that you'd like to modify so you can live more consistently as a Christian?

CONTEMPLATE

Make two lists. On your first list, write down the names of your friends who can most easily support your efforts to live a Christ-centered life. On the second list, write the names of the people who might unintentionally derail your efforts in these areas. How can you work to bring this second group of friends along with you on your journey?

ON SUFFERING

"For it has been granted to you on behalf of Christ not only to believe in him, but also to suffer for him." Philippians 1:29 NIV

All of us have experienced adversity. As I look back over my life, I recall the moments when my business teetered on the edge of failure. I remember the day when I nearly lost my son in a horrific car accident. My darkest day thus far was when my wife died after a short illness. I know others have faced serious tragedies that would seem unimaginable to most of us. When we face these challenges, we often find ourselves questioning why something so terrible could happen to us. In James 1:2-4, we learn that our trials lead to perseverance, making us more complete, not lacking anything.

In this passage, Paul reminds the Philippians that they should consider their suffering as a privilege and an opportunity to grow in Christ. When we face trials in our daily lives, they help us grow spiritually, deepening the relationship we have with Christ. You will find that when you encounter others who have experienced a hardship similar to yours, a bond forms because you can relate to the pain and struggle that person has experienced. You'll see these relationships form among parents who have lost children to drunk driving or gun violence. You'll witness a connection form among those who have struggled with addiction. Paul commends his readers in Philippi for staying true to the teachings of Christ and simultaneously forging a bond amid the persecution they faced.

When you next run up against a seemingly insurmountable challenge, look at it as an opportunity to grow and learn from the experience.

Recall how your previous trials have changed your perspective and deepened your relationship with Christ. Your current suffering can lead to a more fulfilling life in the present and the promise of a rewarding life in eternity.

MY PRAYER

Father, God, help me to embrace my current challenges as opportunities to strengthen my faith and deepen my relationship with you. Let me consider my trials as a privilege and a way to gain a new perspective on a life dedicated to serving you. I pray for these things in the name of your son, Jesus Christ. Amen.

READ: JAMES 1: 2-4

QUESTION #1: What are the trials in your life right now that seem overwhelming?

QUESTION #2: In what ways can you strengthen your faith so that you might more quickly recognize challenges as opportunities for deepening your relationship with Christ?

CONTEMPLATE

Write about a time in your life when a challenge seemed unbearable. How did you grow as a result of that experience and trial?

IDENTITY

"Therefore, if you have any encouragement from being united with Christ, if any comfort from his love, if any common sharing in the Spirit, if any tenderness and compassion, then make my joy complete by being like-minded, having the same love, being one in spirit and of one mind."
Philippians 2:1-2 NIV

The word "identity" can be a trigger these days. In an era of gender fluidity and a constant shaming of masculinity, one's identity can be a controversial subject. As men, we tend to place a lot of value on our occupations, skill levels, and where we fit in the pecking order of society. When we attach our worth to our work, we set the standard too low. Defining ourselves by occupation alone can lead to heartache and frustration. When we make mistakes, lose our jobs or lose interest in things we once thought important, we find ourselves confused about who we are and where we fit in. This could be avoided if we instead found our identity in something constant, pure and perfect: Christ.

One way to discover our true selves is to study God's word for clarity and direction. In 1 Peter 2:9, you'll read that we are a chosen people, a royal priesthood, and God's special possession. I like the sound of those things! After spending time in God's word, you can apply the biblical principles you've learned to guide you in the way you live your life. Once you start living out your new life, your actions—good or bad— will begin to more clearly define you. Allowing yourself to be shaped by who you are in Christ is the best way to find your true identity. Whether you're a brain surgeon or a diesel mechanic, you are infinitely more valuable and wholly unique as a child of God.

You may believe you're unworthy of aligning your identity in Christ. That's the beautiful thing about our sonship. Part of the process of following him is making changes every day to become more like him. In Ephesians 4:20-24, we are taught to put off our old self and to be made new in both our attitude and mind so that we can become more like him. If you're struggling with identity, go to Jesus in prayer and ask him to begin revealing who you are so that you can live according to his will. You'll discover that finding your identity in Christ is easier than trying to be something you could never be.

MY PRAYER

God, help me to surrender my will for what I want my life to look like and embrace my identity through you. Let people see my worth in how I live my life instead of me telling them who I want to be. Let me become worthy of the royal priesthood status you have laid out for me. For these things, I pray in the name of your son, Jesus Christ. Amen.

READ: 2 CORINTHIANS 5:17

QUESTION #1: If someone had asked you about your identity two years ago, how would you have answered the question?

QUESTION #2: If someone asks you about your identity tomorrow, how will you answer the question?

CONTEMPLATE

Write a statement introducing yourself as someone whose identity is found in Christ. How much of your old life still exists in that introduction? How much of your future life is included as part of your identity in Christ?

Do nothing out of selfish ambition or vain conceit. Rather, in humility value others above yourselves, not looking to your own interests but each of you to the interests of the others.

Philippians 2:3-4 NIV

WEEK 3

PUTTING OTHERS FIRST

Do nothing out of selfish ambition or vain conceit. Rather, in humility value others above yourselves, not looking to your own interests but each of you to the interests of the others. Philippians 2:3-4 NIV

When my sons were young, my wife and I sent them to a Christian-themed sports camp in the Missouri Ozarks every summer. They loved going to summer camp and the first question we would always ask after picking them up from the weeklong stay was, "What did you learn at camp this week?"

The answer was always the same. They would say in unison, "God first. Others second. Me third."

My wife and I would nod with approval, hoping this valuable lesson would stay with them for at least the first few hours of our drive home. As our sons became young men, we were pleased they had developed a pattern of putting others first. As a father, I often wondered how I should balance teaching humility against the virtues of assertiveness, mental toughness and being wired to win.

Humility is most easily defined as shifting the focus from your own needs to those of others. As men, it's difficult to remove the focus from ourselves to concentrate on others. If you're like me, part of your DNA is hard-wired with a survival instinct that isn't easy to suppress. Paul challenges us to set aside our pride and ambition and focus on ways to give to others what they need first. As men, we place a high value on comfort, encouragement and social status. Through humility, we should make sure those around us are comfortable, encouraged, and feeling a strong sense of security.

Putting others first doesn't always come naturally. We need to become more intentional in starting with simple gestures of courtesy and kindness when dealing with others. Maybe it starts with letting another driver move into your lane. Perhaps allow someone at the grocery store with fewer items to get in line ahead of you. It could be as easy as stopping for a moment to listen to someone who desperately needs reassurance. Humility can also involve sacrificing something you feel you need for the benefit of another person. Whether your sacrifice is financial, emotional or material, putting another person's needs before your own will always be rewarded in an eternal way.

MY PRAYER

God, help me surrender the instincts that drive my ambition to meet my needs first. Give me a compassionate heart to recognize and honor the needs of others, even when it requires great sacrifice on my part. Let me serve you by serving others. I pray for these things in the name of your son, Jesus Christ. Amen.

READ: MATTHEW 22:36-40

QUESTION #1: What does it mean to be sacrificial in the context of putting others first?

QUESTION #2: In what areas of your life could you more consistently consider putting others' needs before your own?

CONTEMPLATE

Write about a time when another person made a sacrifice to meet your needs. Describe the sacrifice and how you were impacted. What was the outcome?

WEEK

3

DAY

2

HUMILITY

"Who, being in very nature God, did not consider equality with God something to be used to his own advantage; rather, he made himself nothing by taking the very nature of a servant, being made in human likeness." Philippians 2:6-7 NIV

We live in a world where there is a high value placed on success. A man's worth too often is determined by his financial or career success. Younger men might be measured by their physical prowess, skills in the gym, or their ambition. Because we care what the outside world thinks of us, we build up our treasures and accomplishments to establish our place in the social hierarchy. Based on this thinking, we place a disproportionate emphasis on the homes we live in, the vehicles we drive and the number of toys we can pull on a trailer behind our trucks. We somehow believe that the more we have, whether it's money or toys, the more respect we will receive from the outside world. Cultural standards and ideals don't reward men for the virtue of humility.

In the ultimate act of humility, Jesus, the Son of Man, came to this world and gave up his divine privileges to serve mankind. Although he had every right to assert his equality to God, he chose instead to humbly serve humanity. The way he served became core to his mission and teachings, and he set a perfect example for each of us to follow. Jesus demonstrated that the material and physical things of this earth don't count for anything. The treasures that we build up in heaven through love and service to our fellow man are what really matter. Whether it was the act of washing the feet of his disciples or going to extreme measures to serve the least among us, Jesus lived his life on this earth as a servant.

We should be inspired to model Christ in all we do. Demonstrating humility begins with the simple notion of putting others before yourself. More than just a mindset, our actions and deeds will speak volumes about what's truly on our heart. It may be hard to imagine where you can begin serving, so take a moment to consider the least among us. Scripture speaks to the needs of widows, orphans, those who are hungry and those who are without hope. Don't overlook those who simply need encouragement or the benefit of healthy, nurturing relationships. You may have to sacrifice comfort or face resistance to humbly serve, but the end result will always be worth the effort.

MY PRAYER

Heavenly Father, give me the mindset to foster humility in all that I do. Help me to recognize those around me who need my love and service. Help me to overcome the sinful power of pride and arrogance to be a light for others. For these things, I pray in the name of your son, Jesus Christ. Amen.

READ: COLOSSIANS 3:12

QUESTION #1: In what ways can you better demonstrate humility in your daily life?

QUESTION #2: What are the opportunities to serve others that exist within the confines of your church, community or neighborhood?

CONTEMPLATE

Write a journal entry about how to prioritize your responsibilities differently so you can be more intentional about serving, encouraging and working to improve the life of someone in need. Where will you start? Who can you ask to hold you accountable in these efforts?

SPIRITUAL SENSITIVITY

"Therefore, my dear friends, as you have always obeyed—not only in my presence, but now much more in my absence—continue to work out your salvation with fear and trembling, for it is God who works in you to will and to act in order to fulfill his good purpose." Philippians 2:12-13 NIV

If you've ever struggled to lose weight, you understand that shedding pounds typically requires a multifaceted approach. Beyond just consuming fewer calories and eating healthier foods, you often need to increase your daily exercise to help burn calories. You may have to consider the time of day when you're eating, the types of foods that boost your metabolism, and those that slow it down. Unfortunately, there's no magic pill you can take that will melt the pounds. The same is true for our spiritual condition. It takes a multifaceted discipline of obedience to maximize your spiritual sensitivity and fully benefit from the work God wants to do in your life.

In these verses, Paul makes it clear that God is working through each of us to help us achieve our salvation. God is energizing our free will and the corresponding actions all in an effort to tap into his enabling power. He does not take a passive role in our spiritual development. He stays engaged. We can resist his efforts, or we can align ourselves with the work he is doing and be empowered to take bold steps in our Christian walk. As we rely more consistently on our spiritual sensitivity, we begin to get a greater sense of how and where God is leading us.

Recognizing and then embracing what God is doing in our lives will require us to fully surrender our attention to God's will. Once you're open to the idea, you must create a deep desire to recognize all the work being done. This requires a new level of consciousness that most have been ignoring for most of their lives. Being attuned to the Holy Spirit, partaking in fasting, and early morning prayer are practices that can help increase sensitivity. Once you begin to recognize what God is doing, you can become more adeptly tuned to the situations where he is at work. When this happens, we become more obedient in letting God shape our desires and in our readiness to do his will. We can then develop a deep desire to listen intently and attach our hearts to the work God is doing.

MY PRAYER

Father, God, I pray for the discernment and spiritual sensitivity to help me recognize the work that God is doing in my life. Settle my heart and mind so that I can more readily see the pathways being forged on my behalf. For these things, I pray in the name of your son, Jesus Christ. Amen.

READ: ROMANS 8:16-17

QUESTION #1: What steps can you take to increase your spiritual sensitivity to the things God wants to do in your life?

QUESTION #2: What do you suspect God is doing in your life right now?

CONTEMPLATE

Write about a time in your life when you sensed that God was prompting you to take action in a particular area. How did you respond? What was the outcome?

DON'T COMPLAIN

"Do everything without grumbling or arguing, so that you may become blameless and pure, children of God without fault in a warped and crooked generation. Then you will shine among them like stars in the sky."
Philippians 2:14-15 NIV

Early in my business career, I had the good fortune to take the Dale Carnegie Course. Carnegie was a highly respected author and self-improvement guru who wrote many bestselling books, including How to Win Friends and Influence People. While his teachings weren't specifically promoted as Christian-based, it was clear that his faith was at the core of his techniques for improving human relations and achieving professional success. One of the golden rules he promoted in his books was to avoid criticizing, condemning or complaining. By prioritizing positive actions over negative ones, he believed his students could avoid the hazards of resentment and damaged relationships. Carnegie stressed that avoiding negativity in our interactions allows us to be empathetic, giving us a better chance to understand someone else's perspective.

I suspect Carnegie took this lesson from the pages of biblical history and the sage advice the Apostle Paul gave to the Philippians. In addition to the strife that came from the persecution of these early Christians, Paul knew there was also conflict and tension within the group itself. He urged his readers to approach every situation, good or bad, with a positive attitude. Avoiding complaints and arguments would allow them to focus on the important work that needed to be done. By living as a positive example of God's word, his readers could demonstrate God's love through their actions. By taking the high road, they could reflect the true essence of Christ to nonbelievers.

Christians can foster healthy and positive relationships by focusing on the core teachings of Jesus. When we are committed to the foundational principles of forgiveness and reconciliation, we avoid letting our differences fester into something that can destroy relationships. In Mark 12:31, we are told by Jesus that loving our neighbors is among the most important of the commandments. Communicating with one another in an open and honest way will demonstrate the same sense of grace and open heart shown by Jesus. Human relationships can be complicated under almost any circumstances. Staying positive with each other will go a long way toward maintaining peace and building harmony.

MY PRAYER

God, give me the desire to stay positive in my interactions with the people I encounter. Let me reflect the love of Christ in my actions and the way I treat all those around me. Give me the discipline to avoid criticizing, condemning or complaining. For these things I pray in the name of your son, Jesus Christ. Amen.

READ: ROMANS 12:18

QUESTION #1: Why do you believe it feels more natural to criticize and complain instead of staying positive?

QUESTION #2: In which interactions do you have the greatest amount of difficulty staying positive?

CONTEMPLATE

Recall a time when you complained about another person. Revisit those circumstances and write a short paragraph on how you could have handled that situation in a more positive way. Would you expect a different outcome?

BEING SELFLESS

"For everyone looks out for their own interests, not those of Jesus Christ."
Philippians 2:21 NIV

Generally speaking, the male of our species tends to place his own interests above the needs of others. You could blame this behavior on societal expectations as men have historically been assigned to the role of aggressive hunter. As boys, we were conditioned to pursue life with a vigor that placed a strong emphasis on being strong, independent and competitive. Before the era of social promotion, we were taught that there was no trophy awarded for second place. We were recognized for our achievements only if we were the strongest or best in class.

By the time we reach adulthood, men have been told repeatedly that if we want something out of life, we'd better pull up our bootstraps and go get it. Those who succeed are rewarded with the best jobs, the most beautiful companions and the nicest toys. It's hard to shake the reward system that once came with pursuing self-interests. Helping another individual also came with an expectation that we would receive something in return. Times have changed.

In the context of this passage, Paul was praising the selfless nature of Timothy with whom Paul had been in a mentoring relationship for some time. Together, they traveled extensively spreading the gospel. Timothy was a real Boy Scout. He was trustworthy, reliable and loyal. He was selflessly dedicated to the cause of growing God's kingdom. Born to a Greek father and a Jewish mother, Timothy agreed to be circumcised to bolster his credibility with the Jewish community and be a more effective disciple to them. That's commitment! Timothy's salvation was not dependent on this ritual, but it was a sign of his unwavering loyalty to becoming more like Christ. While he would later lead a church in Ephesus, Timothy served the important role as Paul's emissary to the early churches while Paul was imprisoned.

Emulating the life of Timothy begins with a serious examination of the motivations that drive us. Are we willing to set aside our self-interests to address the concerns and missions of God? What does that look like? It begins with a posture of humility, selflessness and compassion that isn't usually recognized by modern society as defining characteristics of a man. If we truly desire to imitate the actions of Paul or Timothy, it will be incumbent upon each of us to seek out opportunities that allow us to serve others with unconditional love and understanding. Putting the needs of others above our own is a hallmark characteristic of men who are pursuing a right relationship with God.

MY PRAYER
God, give me the heart of Timothy. Help me to prioritize the needs of others over my own self-interests. Let me be a loyal and trustworthy servant to God as I endeavor to serve others and spread the gospel. I pray for these things in the name of your son, Jesus Christ. Amen.

READ: I TIMOTHY 4:11-16

QUESTION #1: Compare and contrast your life to that of Timothy. Which of the characteristics of Timothy's life are present in yours?

QUESTION #2: In what areas can you set aside your self-interests to address the needs and concerns of others?

CONTEMPLATE

Make a list of the opportunities in your community to serve those less fortunate. Which of these opportunities has the most appeal to you? Where do you think your talents and interests could have the greatest impact?

"But whatever were gains to me I now consider loss for the sake of Christ. What is more, I consider everything a loss because of the surpassing worth of knowing Christ Jesus my Lord, for whose sake I have lost all things.

Philippians 3:7 NIV

WEEK 4

SERVANT LEADERSHIP

"But I think it is necessary to send back to you Epaphroditus, my brother, co-worker and fellow soldier, who is also your messenger, whom you sent to take care of my needs. For he longs for all of you and is distressed because you heard he was ill. Indeed he was ill, and almost died. But God had mercy on him, and not on him only but also on me, to spare me sorrow upon sorrow. Therefore, I am all the more eager to send him, so that when you see him again you may be glad and I may have less anxiety. So then, welcome him in the Lord with great joy, and honor people like him, because he almost died for the work of Christ. He risked his life to make up for the help you yourselves could not give me." Philippians 2:25-30 NIV

When you think back about the best boss you ever worked for, consider the attributes and characteristics that make you remember him or her in such a positive way. I've had a lot of bosses over the years and some were pretty lousy. My worst bosses got caught up in the status and power of their position. My best bosses took a genuine interest in me and actively sought ways to help me succeed. But the leaders who had the greatest influence over me were not my bosses but rather my peers who stepped forward at inconvenient times and did the hard work no one else wanted to do.

In this passage, Paul draws attention to a true servant leader named Epaphroditus, who dared greatly and made significant sacrifice to advance the cause of Christianity on behalf of the Philippians. Epaphroditus was the messenger sent from Philippi to deliver funds that had been raised to support Paul's missionary work while he was imprisoned in Rome. On his journey, Epaphroditus became gravely ill and nearly died but kept moving to make sure Paul received the support he needed. It's not often that we encounter leaders who selflessly risk life and limb in the service of others. When someone steps forward and is willing to sacrifice in this manner for a greater cause, it's noteworthy.

Epaphroditus had the essential attributes that transform an ordinary boss into a servant leader. He was selfless, empathetic, compassionate and caring. In a similar manner, Jesus showed his stripes as a leader when he decided to wash the feet of his disciples. As the Son of Man, he had every right to be served, but he chose to serve instead. Servant leaders serve their subordinates well when they empower and support them in ways that help them grow and succeed. Servant leaders are open and transparent and place a high value on trust, honesty and grace. When leaders focus on relationships rather than responsibility, they earn a sense of loyalty and respect that most bosses will never experience.

MY PRAYER

God, give me the heart of a servant leader. Help me to be mindful of the attributes that I must demonstrate before gaining the trust and confidence to lead others. Above all things, give me the tools I need to more frequently and effectively lead others to you. For these things, I pray in the name of your son, Jesus Christ. Amen.

READ: MARK 10:42-45

QUESTION #1: What are the words you would use to describe your leadership style?

QUESTION #2: What were the characteristics of the leader you consider your favorite boss?

CONTEMPLATE

Write about the opportunities you have to lead other men. What skills or personality traits can you strengthen to become a more effective leader?

DECEPTION

"Watch out for those dogs, those evildoers, those mutilators of the flesh. For it is we who are the circumcision, we who serve God by his Spirit, who boast in Christ Jesus, and who put no confidence in the flesh."
Philippians 3:2-3 NIV

In his letter to the Philippians, Paul reminded his readers that their righteousness is not based on their own works, but solely because of their faith in Jesus Christ. Regardless of their merit, good deeds and compassionate actions, they were in good standing with God because of Jesus's sacrifice on the cross. This, of course, was a contrary message to that of false teachers and Judaizers in Philippi who were telling them they could not be justified in God's sight without adhering to Jewish rituals and traditions laid out in Old Testament law and the Torah. At the heart of the issue was this question: Must a man be circumcised before being considered righteous?

As you might surmise from the tone and directness of Paul's words, the deception and ulterior motives of these false teachers frustrated him. At one point, Paul compared the Judaizers to a pack of wild dogs that would kill and deceive to get what they wanted. Paul pointed out the absurdity of salvation being reliant on an ancient ritual that involves mutilating your body. He insisted that a "true circumcision" was more a spiritual transformation than a physical act against the body.

If someone has ever purposely misled you, you can relate to the disappointment Paul felt on behalf of these new Christians. Even today, it's hard for many to believe that God's promise of eternal life is real. That's what is so incredibly powerful about God's love for us. To be justified, we simply must believe that Jesus's life was sacrificed to atone for our sin. We must confess our sins to God so we can graciously receive the forgiveness that came with God sending us his son. To honor this commitment, we should strive to perfect our faith and live lives worthy of the sacrifice that was made on our behalf.

MY PRAYER

Father, God, make me vigilant in protecting my heart and mind from those who wish to deceive and steal what God has graciously given to me. Help me absorb the truth and share it with others so that they will know that our salvation is only possible through our faith in the sacrifice of Christ Jesus. Amen.

READ: EPHESIANS 2:8-9

QUESTION #1: What do you believe is the reason for your salvation?

QUESTION #2: Why is God's promise of salvation such a hard concept for so many people to believe?

CONTEMPLATE

Write a brief letter to a nonbeliever explaining what is required to become a follower of Christ. What words will you use to assure them of this promise?

COMMON GROUND

"Though I myself have reasons for such confidence. If someone else thinks they have reasons to put confidence in the flesh, I have more: circumcised on the eighth day, of the people of Israel, of the tribe of Benjamin, a Hebrew of Hebrews; in regard to the law, a Pharisee; as for zeal, persecuting the church; as for righteousness based on the law, faultless."
Philippians 3:4-6 NIV

When it came to proving his pedigree as a Jew, the Apostle Paul boasted an impressive resume. Per Jewish tradition and God's command to Abraham, Paul was circumcised when he was eight days old. He was a member of the Tribe of Benjamin, one of two remaining tribes that had stayed loyal to David. He was a citizen of Israel and diligent in observing Hebrew law and culture. Paul described himself as a "Pharisee of Pharisees" to show his zealousness for Judaism. His strict adherence to Mosaic Law through much of his life cemented his credibility with those Jews who were strongly questioning his claims about Christ.

Oddly, Paul wasn't bragging about his credentials as a Jew. His intent was to make the case that he deeply understood the tenets of Jewish traditions and laws. He wanted those who challenged him to understand that he had a baseline understanding and common ground with those who challenged his way of thinking. Their salvation would not be determined by their deeds or by their adherence to Mosaic Law, but rather by coming to faith because of the selfless act of Jesus dying on the cross. Because of their common heritage, Paul had the best chance of bridging the gap between Judaism and Christianity. Fortunately, Paul had unusual access to Jewish communities and synagogues, giving him a chance to share the gospel and good news of Christ.

If you've ever struggled to find common ground with a nonbeliever, you can relate to Paul's frustrations. In the end, Paul was able to use Old Testament scripture to demonstrate that Jesus was the fulfillment of Jewish prophecies. While starting with opposite viewpoints, they found unity by focusing first on the areas where they agreed. As disciples, we must be willing to invest the time and effort required to get to know and understand others with differing perspectives on faith. Rather than casting them aside with hopeless abandon, we must commit to the hard work of forging relationships based on trust and compassion through service. Our ability to show others that salvation is possible only because of God's grace is not based on our pedigree as Christians but in the way we demonstrate what's on our hearts in the service of Christ.

MY PRAYER

God, give me the compassion to find common ground with those who do not believe in you. Grant me the perseverance of Paul in my work and the heart I need to make the case for Christ. I pray for these things in the name of your son, Jesus Christ. Amen.

READ: GALATIANS 1:13-24

QUESTION #1: What steps can you take to find common ground with nonbelievers?

QUESTION #2: How can you better equip yourself make the case for Christ?

CONTEMPLATE

Think of a person you know who is skeptical about Christianity. Make a list of the areas of common ground you might have with that person. In what ways can you establish a sense of unity with this person?

KNOWING CHRIST

"But whatever were gains to me I now consider loss for the sake of Christ. What is more, I consider everything a loss because of the surpassing worth of knowing Christ Jesus my Lord, for whose sake I have lost all things. I consider them garbage, that I may gain Christ and be found in him, not having a righteousness of my own that comes from the law, but that which is through faith in Christ—the righteousness that comes from God on the basis of faith." Philippians 3:7-9 NIV

As a young man, I invested a lot of time building up my resume. I spent hours compiling lists of accomplishments, proficiencies and skill sets to prove that I was more than qualified for any job I pursued. To demonstrate that I was also a decent human being, I put together a list of the volunteer work I had done as well as a list of the boards and commissions on which I had served. When I transitioned into politics, you can only imagine the detail that went into my long list of "attaboys!" On paper, I looked like a great guy. Looking back, all that effort seems like a waste of time. If I had put the same energy into my spiritual pursuits, my long-term gain would have been immeasurable.

Paul went to great lengths to make certain his enemies knew the depth of his Jewish pedigree. His work on behalf of the gospel was also undisputed. He had nothing to prove to anyone. Yet, Paul made it clear to his readers that his list of attributes was nothing more than garbage when compared to the value he derived from his relationship with Christ. Paul traded a comfortable seat in the temple for the bars and chains of prison. He gave up his freedom as a privileged citizen. He had nothing left to lose or gain at that point in his life. In the final analysis, finding his identity in Christ was all that mattered to Paul.

I once heard a Christian speaker remind his audience to "keep the main thing the main thing." The main thing, he said, is our relationship with Christ. Nothing else matters. When I think back on all the sacrifices I made in building my business, my career and net worth, I am saddened to realize that there will be a day when I have nothing to show for that hard work. On my day of judgment, no one will ask to see my resume. They won't care how high I climbed up the corporate ladder. But there will be an accounting of the treasure I have built up in heaven. I am grateful that I still have an opportunity to make more deposits in that effort. God willing, I can spend the remainder of my days building something that will be of eternal importance.

MY PRAYER

God, give me an eternal focus that takes my attention from the things of this earth to a deeper relationship with you. Give me the confidence I need to stop pleasing my peers in this world and to start doing the work that matters beyond this life. For these things, I pray in the name of your son, Jesus Christ. Amen.

READ: MATTHEW 6:19-21

QUESTION #1: Why do you believe Paul valued his relationship with Christ over the many accomplishments he experienced as a disciple for Christ?

QUESTION #2: What can you do today to start building up your treasures in heaven?

CONTEMPLATE

Write a journal entry about the ways you would like to see your relationship with Christ evolve over the coming weeks and months. What will change about your relationship? What will you do differently to enhance this relationship?

BE RESILIENT

"Brothers and sisters, I do not consider myself yet to have taken hold of it. But one thing I do: Forgetting what is behind and straining toward what is ahead, I press on toward the goal to win the prize for which God has called me heavenward in Christ Jesus." Philippians 3:13-14 NIV

For most of us, the Christian journey is not a sprint, but a long marathon filled with setbacks and challenges that can make the goal seem distant. Just when we think we have it all figured out, something derails our progress. My Christian walk has consistently been about moving three steps forward and falling two steps back. The cumulative result is still a positive gain but at a painstakingly slow pace. Unfortunately, some of our brothers will never make it past the starting block. We can be so haunted by our past mistakes and the harm we have caused ourselves and others that we are paralyzed by our fears and thoughts of unworthiness.

Paul uses this passage to acknowledge that he has not achieved perfection in his Christian walk. He stresses the need to forget what is in your past and keep forging ahead toward your ultimate aim. Our path to Christ is much like any other goal that we set for ourselves. Finding success requires discipline, obedience and a steadfast pursuit of what matters most. We have plans in place for our financial independence, fitness goals and career. It makes sense that we take the same approach for our spiritual objectives.

Being resilient in your spiritual pursuits starts with first reflecting on your transgressions and going through the process of forgiving yourself. Know that you're not alone in making serious mistakes in your life.

You are blessed to serve a God who has already forgiven you for your sins. Next, identify the areas in your life where you'd like to grow as a Christian, and set specific goals along with action items that will help you achieve them. This is difficult to accomplish on your own. You can invite a trusted friend or spiritual mentor to walk alongside you, holding you accountable for the steps you have promised to take. If you're willing to invest the same effort in your spiritual development that you do in other areas of your life, there's no doubt that you will be on the right path right away.

MY PRAYER

Father, teach me to be resilient in all that I do. Help me set aside my past mistakes and look to a future where my eternal life with you is my most coveted prize. Give me courage to forgive myself and then the discipline and obedience to run the race that brings me closer to you. I pray for these things in the name of your son, Jesus Christ. Amen.

READ: ISAIAH 40:30-31

QUESTION #1: Are there things in your past for which you need to forgive yourself before moving forward? What are those things?

QUESTION #2: What is an example of something you have achieved in your life that required discipline and obedience?

CONTEMPLATE

Write a journal entry outlining the spiritual objectives you want to achieve. Identify those which should be an immediate priority.

"Do not be anxious about anything, but in every situation, by prayer and petition, with thanksgiving, present your requests to God. And the peace of God, which transcends all understanding, will guard your hearts and your minds in Christ Jesus."

Philippians 4:6-7 NIV

WEEK 5

SPIRITUAL MATURITY

"All of us, then, who are mature should take such a view of things. And if on some point you think differently, that too God will make clear to you. Only let us live up to what we have already attained." Philippians 3:15-16 NIV

If you've attended many weddings, you've heard messages about love that come from 1 Corinthians 13. In particular, you may remember the passage that reads, "When I was a child, I spoke like a child, I thought like a child, I reasoned like a child; when I became a man, I put away childish things." Spiritual maturity is measured in a variety of ways, but Paul wanted the Philippians to know that once they came to understand God's nature and the teachings of Jesus, it was important to lead lives that honored this knowledge. Paul encouraged these new Christians to be confident in what they knew and that when disagreements inevitably arose, God would reveal the truth to them.

One of my struggles when I began my Christian walk was my lack of understanding of the full breadth of God's word. I was raised Catholic and was never encouraged to spend much time in the Bible. While I understood the basic tenets of Christianity and the New Testament stories of Christ, I didn't understand how it all influenced the way I lived my life. As I began to spend a few minutes each day studying scripture, the pieces of the big puzzle started to come together. Though I once dreaded the contents of the Old Testament, I discovered how the prophecies outlined in those books made the compelling case for Christ. It was a painfully slow process for me until I developed a curiosity about scripture that left me thirsty for more knowledge.

When we become more mature as Christians, we are expected to live in a way that reflects that. Paul hopes that our behavior will more closely mirror God's character as we navigate the emotional highs and lows of life's circumstances. As we grow, we will live more consistently with humility and stronger self-awareness. We will understand ourselves better and be able to moderate our reactions more easily. We won't be content with mediocrity in our spiritual pursuits and will yearn for something beyond our current understanding. When it all comes together, we will begin to align our minds and hearts with the goal of becoming more like Christ in all that we do.

MY PRAYER

God, give me an eagerness to become more spiritually mature. Help me shape my thoughts and behaviors so that I might live a life that more closely aligns with Christ. I pray for these things in the name of your son, Jesus Christ. Amen.

READ: EPHESIANS 4:14-15

QUESTION #1: How would you rate your current level of spiritual maturity?

QUESTION #2: What changes could you make to your lifestyle and daily habits that would assist in your efforts to become more like Christ?

CONTEMPLATE

Write a journal entry that describes the benchmark moments of your Christian walk. At what points along the way did you mature spiritually? What does the future of your spiritual development look like?

WORTH FOLLOWING

"Join together in following my example, brothers and sisters, and just as you have us as a model, keep your eyes on those who live as we do. For, as I have often told you before and now tell you again even with tears, many live as enemies of the cross of Christ." Philippians 3:17-18 NIV

We've all known people who will preach one thing and turn around and do something contrary to the principle they just espoused. We often refer to these people as hypocrites because their words don't match their actions. Unfortunately, too many of us have encountered hypocrites in our early church experiences. The Apostle Paul's words, actions and attitudes were consistent with his heart and his obedience to God. His word was his bond, he set a wonderful example, and he expected the same high standards from those who followed him. Putting on outward appearances wasn't good enough; Paul demanded that his new Christians live in a way that reflected the values of Christ.

When you reflect on the life of Paul, you know he was steadfast in his beliefs and unshakable in his convictions. Starting with his encounter with Christ on the road to Damascus, Paul humbled himself and spent his life serving and putting the needs of others before his own. Along the way, he endured significant hardships from beatings to imprisonment, but he stayed true to his mission to spread the word of God. Though he could have lived a life of extreme privilege, he chose to defend and elevate those whom society had cast aside. He showed the same compassion for those he referred to as "enemies of the cross," who worked against his efforts.

In an era when there is a dearth of positive male role models, we can be inspired by the life of Paul and emulate the values he modeled more than 2,000 years ago. There are still opportunities for us to be bold about our faith and share the good news with anyone who will listen. We can ferociously present and defend the truth in the moments when it matters most. And, of course, there remain plenty of ways to serve others. When your life imitates the way Paul lived his life, you will be met with the kind of resistance he encountered in the early days of the church. But anything worth having is worth fighting for. Living a life that honors God is one of those things.

MY PRAYER

God, inspire me to live like Paul. Give me the courage to have his convictions and the heart to love others as he did. Let me be steadfast and unwavering in my beliefs and willing to endure the hardships that may come with living a Christ-like life. For these things, I pray in the name of your son, Jesus Christ.

READ: HEBREWS 11

QUESTION #1: In what area of your life are your words out of alignment with your actions or behavior?

QUESTION #2: In what ways could you be more steadfast in your convictions?

CONTEMPLATE

Make a list of the areas in your life where you could humble yourself to better serve others. What will you do to get started?

LIVING AS A REFUGEE

"But our citizenship is in heaven. And we eagerly await a Savior from there, the Lord Jesus Christ," Philippians 3:20 NIV

When a large group of Burmese refugees came to our town several years ago, my wife was one of the first people to step forward and help these newcomers acclimate to our community and American culture. She often talked of the hardships and complexities these individuals faced because of being displaced from their homeland, many with only the clothes on their backs. Navigating limited housing options, school systems, and employment opportunities was a daunting task. Language barriers and our deep reliance on technology made the transition more difficult. While these exiles were grateful for their new home, they longed for the food, traditions and familial relationships of their native home.

As Christians, we should be mindful that we are, in many respects, refugees living for a short time in a foreign land. This earth is not our permanent home. The hardships and difficulties we face are temporary and will seem inconsequential once we arrive at our new home in heaven. Knowing this, it's important to remember that we should not conform to the ways of this world for they are rife with sin and our comfort here only separates us from God. Instead, we must keep our allegiances focused on the customs and traditions of our eternal home, which is with God.

Unlike the refugees who have come to America, our citizenship in heaven is guaranteed. Once we've accepted Jesus, there are no forms to fill out, hurdles to jump or bureaucracies to navigate. Until that day comes, we should continue to live as strangers in a foreign land, rejecting the things that the rest of the world is trying to push on us. Conforming to the ways of this world has no eternal benefit to us. Living differently from everyone else may bring a temporary discomfort, but being countercultural in a world filled with sin can be a positive thing. Our reward will come when we cross the border to our permanent homeland with a passport that has been stamped with the precious blood of Jesus Christ.

MY PRAYER

God, help me keep my focus on the customs and traditions of my permanent home in heaven. Give me the discipline I need to be obedient and to resist conforming to the patterns of this sinful world. For these things, I pray in the name of your son, Jesus Christ. Amen.

READ: JOHN 14:1-14

QUESTION #1: What steps can you take to resist conforming to the patterns of this world?

QUESTION #2: What customs and traditions in this world can help you prepare for your life in your eternal home?

CONTEMPLATE

Make a list of the things in this world that entrap you in sin. What steps can you take to resist this sin? What do you believe will be your biggest challenges in this area?

CROWNING ACHIEVEMENT

"Therefore, my brothers and sisters, you whom I love and long for, my joy and crown, stand firm in the Lord in this way, dear friends!" Philippians 4:1 NIV

Have you ever worked hard to achieve something and when it finally came to fruition, you felt like you had conquered the world? Perhaps your crowning achievement was completing your education, running a marathon, or being promoted at work. Perhaps your victory came in the form of saving your marriage, reconciling with an estranged relative, or beating an addiction. You felt a sense of pride and realized that all the hard work was worth the reward. In this passage to the Philippians, Paul found immense joy in seeing the progress these early Christians made despite extraordinarily difficult circumstances.

If you've been involved in planting a church or have participated in a tight-knit Bible study group, you've probably discovered the bond created when a small group of believers comes together and commits to obediently follow Christ. When this happens, you inevitably share the trials and triumphs that come from living a Christ-centered life. As a family, you forge the mountains and valleys of life in a community that supports one another through joys and sorrows. Paul felt that same bond with the Philippians. Their willingness to sacrifice their own comfort to support the spread of Christianity into other parts of the world felt like a major victory for Paul.

Paul encouraged these new believers to stand firm in their faith so that they could continue to grow, no matter how difficult the circumstances. Standing firm meant resisting evil influences that would lure them into temptation, expose them to false teachings and subject them to further persecution. By growing stronger in their faith, they would discover that their true citizenship was in heaven rather than on this Earth. Laboring side by side with Paul and other believers, they would one day receive their crowning achievement ... a just reward for a life of faithfulness and radical obedience.

MY PRAYER

Give me the vision I need to see the reward that comes with steadfast faithfulness and the sacrifice of comfort in my daily life. Let me find Paul's joy in working beside fellow believers with the common goal of glorifying your kingdom. For these things, I pray in the name of your son, Jesus Christ. Amen.

READ: JAMES 1:12

QUESTION #1: What is the accomplishment in your life of which you are most proud?

QUESTION #2: In what ways do you motivate yourself to remain steadfast in pursuit of your goals?

CONTEMPLATE

Create a journal entry about something you accomplished with God's help. What were the obstacles you had to overcome to forge ahead? How did God help you persist?

GENTLENESS

"Rejoice in the Lord always. I will say it again: Rejoice! Let your gentleness be evident to all. The Lord is near." Philippians 4:4-5 NIV

One of the most influential factors during the initial stages of my Christian journey was being in the presence of men who seemed content and joyful in their lives. When someone would ask them the reason for their joy and satisfaction with life's circumstances, they inevitably would mention their relationship with Jesus. Their answers became a powerful testimony to the good that God can do in a man's life. Those of us who have achieved any level of spiritual maturity should feel duty-bound to demonstrate the joy and gentleness that come from living a Christ-centered life.

Paul instructs us to let our "gentleness be evident" to all we encounter. Gentleness is not a characteristic typically assigned to men. We are most often measured by our strength, physical appearance, intellect or net worth. Though men of good character are often referred to as "gentlemen," the derivative of this term has nothing to do with what it truly means to be gentle. The idea of being gentle is contrary to what many expect from the male species. From the time most of us were young boys, people tolerated and, at times, encouraged our rambunctious behavior and horseplay. There is nothing gentle about the way men interact with each other. Once again, Paul is calling us to rise up and stand out from the crowd and live our lives in a manner that is extraordinary … not ordinary.

Because gentleness is one of the fruits of the Holy Spirit, we know that we have all been blessed with this gift. A gentle man is respectful, considerate and puts the needs and interests of others first. He is the opposite of stubborn. He exercises self-control, humility and is quick to forgive. He listens to the viewpoints of others and remains calm, even when he disagrees with their opinions. He understands that he is not in control. He knows that his destiny is determined only by God and for that reason, he focuses his energies on pleasing God. His joy is constant, even during tough times, because the foundation of his happiness is in Christ. He always treats others with grace, a true reflection of the God he serves.

MY PRAYER

God, help me to live my life in a manner where people want to know the reason for my joy. Give me the heart and mind of a gentle man, reflecting your goodness and grace in all that I do. I pray for these things in the name of your son, Jesus Christ. Amen.

READ: GALATIANS 5:22-23

QUESTION #1: In what areas of your life, can you demonstrate gentleness with others?

QUESTION #2: In what ways can you exercise gentleness in the presence of those you encounter regularly?

CONTEMPLATE

Make a list of the men you've known throughout your life who were gentle. Was their masculinity in question because of their gentle nature? How can you model your life to be more like these men?

*"I am not saying this because I am in need,
for I have learned to be content whatever
the circumstances. I know what it is to be in need,
and I know what it is to have plenty."*

Philippians 4:11 NIV

WEEK 6

ANXIETY

"Do not be anxious about anything, but in every situation, by prayer and petition, with thanksgiving, present your requests to God. And the peace of God, which transcends all understanding, will guard your hearts and your minds in Christ Jesus." Philippians 4:6-7 NIV

In my work with young adults, I've discovered that we're bringing up an entire generation that struggles with anxiety. Recent studies suggest that nearly 40% of adolescents battle an anxiety disorder. There's no rational explanation for this sudden increase among young people other than what many experts attribute to the prevalence of social media and other societal changes over the last two decades. All of us have experienced various levels of anxiety in our lives, but it's hard to imagine living with a disorder that dominates such a large part of a person's life. Of course, some cases of anxiety require professional counseling.

Not to diminish the havoc it plays on young lives, but I wonder if we, in our yearning to be tolerant, have allowed anxiety to become an acceptable sin. Paul's words to the Philippians are clear. We are to give our worries and troubles over to God with prayer and thanksgiving. We can't expect God to take away our anxieties, but we can be confident that God will see us through them. In 1 Peter 5:7, we are told to cast all our cares on God because he cares for us. Not trusting God with our worries is a sin.

I suppose that the parenting skills of many Baby Boomers and Gen Xers could be to blame for this problem. As parents, we mistakenly wanted to spare our children from the pain and disappointment we experienced in our adolescence. In retrospect, we denied our children the opportunity to create coping mechanisms to deal with tough situations. The best thing we can do now is encourage our children and grandchildren to lean into their relationships with God and seek peace and guidance from God through the most challenging times. If you struggle with anxiety, consider sharing your concerns with fellow believers and make a daily practice of replacing negative thoughts with God-centered perspectives that are forward-looking and built on a foundation of gratitude.

MY PRAYER

Father, God, thank you for allowing me to cast my cares upon you. Help me be mindful that you welcome my concerns and that you will see me through them. Bless those among us who struggle with anxiety, bring them the same peace that you bring into my life. For these things, I pray in the name of your son, Jesus Christ. Amen.

READ: PSALMS 23

QUESTION #1: What is preventing you from turning over your worries and concerns to God?

QUESTION #2: How can you assist others struggling with anxiety? What can you tell them about God?

CONTEMPLATE

Make a list of the things that cause worry or concern in your life. How many of these concerns have you entrusted to God? How many of these concerns could be added to your daily prayers?

MINDSET

"Finally, brothers and sisters, whatever is true, whatever is noble, whatever is right, whatever is pure, whatever is lovely, whatever is admirable—if anything is excellent or praiseworthy—think about such things." Philippians 4:8 NIV

I f you've heard the phrase, "Garbage in, garbage out," you already know that our thoughts and behaviors are influenced by our mindset and the content we absorb from our environment and those around us. If the things we view and listen to throughout the day are negative, there's an excellent chance our thoughts and actions will be negative. Paul tells us that if our mind is focused on wholesome things, our disposition will likewise be influenced. We all know people who tend to have a positive outlook on life. These folks tend to believe their life will be filled with a preponderance of good things, and indeed they tend to live out a pretty blessed life.

In this passage, Paul encourages his readers in Philippi to take an active role in resolving the conflict that has arisen between two women in the church. He tells his readers to focus on only the good things in life. Of course, eliminating that conflict would allow these new Christians to shift their attention toward the more positive things that please God. Paul encourages them to focus exclusively on all that is pure and lovely. If there is something that is extraordinary or worthy of praise, the Philippians are called to focus on those things. To make it stick, Paul encourages these new Christians to continually dwell on these positive things.

Living our lives in this manner would be a radical change for most of us. Our human nature has us dwelling only on the things we don't have or the situations in our lives that we can't control. Because God wants us to be good stewards of our choices and he has given us the ability to control our mind's focus. He has also given us the will to choose the people we trust and the ability to take deliberate actions in the areas where we can make a difference. One of the best ways to maintain a positive mindset that is pleasing to God is to keep track of the things in your life for which you are grateful. You should record this list of things in a gratitude journal and update it as frequently as you can. Perhaps you're grateful for a loving marriage, healthy children and a stable career. By making the effort to acknowledge these things daily, you are responding well to God's request to focus on the good things in this life.

MY PRAYER

God, give me a mindset that allows me to focus on all that is good in this world. Give me the discernment to recognize that which is excellent and worthy of praise. Give me the obedience to dwell on only good things. For all these things, I pray in the name of your son, Jesus Christ. Amen.

READ: ROMANS 12:2

QUESTION #1: What are the good and positive things that you've experienced in recent days?

QUESTION #2: What prevents you from dwelling only on the positive things in your world?

CONTEMPLATE

Make a list of 20 things for which you are grateful. Place an asterisk next to the items on your list that you believe may be unique to your life. How challenging would it be to add additional items to this list each day?

BEING CONTENT

"I am not saying this because I am in need, for I have learned to be content whatever the circumstances. I know what it is to be in need, and I know what it is to have plenty. I have learned the secret of being content in any and every situation, whether well fed or hungry, whether living in plenty or in want." Philippians 4:11-12 NIV

In my life, I've had the opportunity to know some extraordinarily successful people. One thing that stands out to me is that some of the wealthiest people I know are also some of the unhappiest people I know. It's uncanny. Most people assume that their problems would go away if they just had enough money. You've probably heard the adage that "money can't buy you happiness," but there's something inside each of us that still wants to find out for sure. The easy answer to man's elusive search for joy and contentment is that they can be found in a relationship with Christ.

Have you ever known someone who seemed content? If you have, you know that there's something different about them. They don't get too worried about what other people are doing or saying. They don't get hot and bothered when someone gets something they didn't deserve. Truly content people have a sense of peace about them because they are experiencing the fullness of Christ and that's all that matters to them. We should envy that. We should be drawn to them. We should want what they have. Imagine how effective we would be in bringing others to Christ if only they could see the peace and contentment in him. We can get there if we're willing to prioritize our relationship with him, actively seeking his will and following his teachings. Experiencing the true fullness of Christ will lead us to a life of contentment we never could have imagined.

Despite Paul's longstanding suffering and trials, he found contentment in his relationship with Christ. He didn't have comfort, wealth, good health or a happy family at home, but his sense of peace and joy was perpetual. Paul's contentment transcended his circumstances. His joy came in knowing Christ and finding his identity there. Most of us believe we could find contentment if only we could be free of debt or free from a toxic relationship. Our happiness will not come from this kind of freedom. It can only come from a total dependence on Christ. We can discover this for ourselves if we lean into what God is offering us and know that nothing else will even come close. The search is over.

MY PRAYER

God, help me discover the contentment that can come only through my relationship with you. Help me seek a joy that is authentic and pure and not tied to material possessions or status. Let my focus be on growing in you and becoming the best version of myself. I pray for these things in the name of your son, Jesus Christ. Amen.

READ: HEBREWS 13:5

QUESTION #1: What efforts have you made in the past to find contentment and joy in your life? What was the outcome?

QUESTION #2: What steps can you take to grow closer to Christ so that your contentment comes from within instead of from external circumstances?

CONTEMPLATE

Write a journal entry describing what your life will look like once you find joy and contentment. How will you get there? What obstacles are preventing you from being content?

GROWTH IN SUFFERING

"I can do all this through him who gives me strength."
Philippians 4:13 NIV

When you mature as a Christian, you begin to understand that suffering is an integral part of the journey. Life can be tough. We are all going to suffer at times. Whether your suffering stems from something as common as financial hardships or marital discourse or something life-changing, like the sudden loss of a loved one, it's a natural part of life. In James 1:2-6, we learn that difficult times can be beneficial to our spiritual development and resolve. Suffering strengthens our faith through perseverance and gives us hope.

Although this Bible verse may be the one most often taken out of its proper context, there's still a powerful message found within its words. Paul's intent was to remind his readers that God equipped us to endure anything that comes our way. No matter the hardship or severity of persecution, God has given us what we need to survive and we will benefit in some measure from the experience. It is during these most difficult moments we discover that God has our back. No matter how terrible the circumstances, we will find reassurance. We will grow in some way. We will learn something about ourselves that we didn't think was possible.

The most important lesson you can take away from this short verse is in learning that you are not without power, regardless of the trials you face. God gives you what you need to get through your troubles. He has equipped you to withstand temptation and he has given you the power to endure even the worst tragedy. With these few words, you will have the confidence to know you can stand firm, pursue a Godly life, and take whatever risks you feel are necessary to live a full life. Rather than living in dread of the terrible things that might happen, live with the confidence and satisfaction that God will protect and strengthen you as you endeavor to become the best version of yourself.

MY PRAYER

God, let me cling to the confidence of knowing you are here to help me endure any trial that may come my way. Help me to embrace my suffering as an opportunity for growth and spiritual development. I pray for these things in the name of your son, Jesus Christ. Amen.

READ: JEREMIAH 32:17

QUESTION #1: How difficult is it for you to embrace your suffering and regard it as an opportunity for growth?

QUESTION #2: What has been the most significant trial of your life?

CONTEMPLATE

Recall a recent challenge that seemed overwhelming at the time and then describe how you grew from that experience. Were you able to feel God's presence at any point during this difficult period?

RECEIVING GRACIOUSLY

"I have received full payment and have more than enough. I am amply supplied, now that I have received from Epaphroditus the gifts you sent. They are a fragrant offering, an acceptable sacrifice, pleasing to God."
Philippians 4:18 NIV

Sometimes it's hard to be a gracious receiver. Often, our pride keeps us from accepting gifts in the spirit in which they were intended. Even when we're down and out and have nowhere else to turn for help, we can find it difficult to accept another person's generosity, no matter how small. For some of us, there's a degree of shame that comes with needing help, let alone accepting it. When a neighbor offers a meal, free babysitting, or something as common as a gift from their garden, most of us don't know how to accept the gift graciously. We respond by saying, "Oh, we're fine. That's not necessary. You didn't need to do that."

Instead of feeling disrespected by the gesture, we should pay attention to the heart of the giver. When a person gives generously, they receive a reciprocal blessing in knowing their kindness is pleasing to God. The satisfaction that comes from helping others is a remarkable feeling that can be an extraordinary blessing. In nearly every case, God takes care of the givers by fulfilling their needs in return. Granted, generosity is not something that should ever be governed by a quid pro quo relationship where some consideration is expected in return. Giving is only considered an act of worship when absolutely nothing is expected in return. I can now understand why so many generous givers do so anonymously or perform their acts of kindness when no one else is looking.

The best way to accept another person's generosity is to accept it with grace. Know that their heart is in the right place. There's so much joy that comes from giving with a selfless heart and the best way to humbly accept a gift is simply to say, "Thank you!" The grace you demonstrate in receiving a gift is the best way to show appreciation for the providence of God. In 2 Corinthians 9:11, we discover that the best response to a gift is to give thanks to God for the circumstances that made it possible and to take comfort in knowing he will replenish resources and provide for the generous giver, just as he has provided for you.

MY PRAYER

God, teach me to become a gracious recipient of your grace and the generosity of others. Help me recognize that acts of kindness and generosity are made possible only by you. May I be blessed to give as abundantly as I have received. For these things, we pray in the name of your son, Jesus Christ. Amen.

READ: 2 CORINTHIANS 9: 10-11

QUESTION #1: What steps can you take to become a more gracious recipient of the kindness and generosity of others?

QUESTION #2: How can you teach your heart to give more graciously while expecting nothing in return?

CONTEMPLATE

Make a list of the blessings you have received from others who have expected nothing in return. How did you acknowledge their kindness? What have you learned from these experiences?

15 RULES OF ENGAGEMENT FOR SMALL-GROUP STUDIES

1. Nothing said in the group gets discussed outside the group!

2. Be transparent. Be authentic. Be your true self.

3. Everyone needs to share, both as a speaker and a listener.

4. Encourage one another. Speak truth into each others' lives avoiding the temptation to "fix" each other.

5. Challenge each other. It's reasonable to disagree, but respect boundaries.

6. Give your darkest issues the light of day. It's incredibly liberating!

7. Be willing to be vulnerable. Take a chance and let your risk be rewarded.

8. We all have blind spots. Dare to explore your own.

9. Absolutely NO gossip.

10. Embrace your mistakes. Take ownership of your weaknesses, knowing that we're all human.

11. Resist the urge to rescue others when they struggle to find the right words. Let people finish their thoughts.

12. Don't be afraid of silence. Pause and feel the weight of what has been shared.

13. Trust is our most important currency. Earn it and then be willing to extend trust to others.

14. Side conversations are a sign of disrespect; only one voice at a time.

15. When possible, find time to connect with each other outside the small group setting.

·